POOL STAKER

AN ETHAN WARES SKATEBOARD SERIES
BOOK 3

MARK MAPSTONE

1

THE FOUNTAIN OF DEATH

If you wanted to find zombies, simply head for the library. Those who began as fresh, imaginative, playful children would, over time, become a subdued white noise of dull adults. Life drained of blood, slow-moving soulless corpses.

The doom-factory didn't start out that way. Designed by Spanish architect, Maria De Soto Mayor, this blood-red building poked out of the tombstone grey horizon of shabby retail premises and thrust its goth-black A-frame spires into the clouds, as if Death itself needed a boundary fence. Its walls met the ground with tiny transitions which flowed into an organic brick pump-track as if it had tree roots spanning out in search of food. It pulled in anything with a pulse towards its tiny, boring mouth with a ray of stupid sunshine.

The only people it couldn't devour were the

skaters. The inside never appealed when the outside was so incredible.

In the centre of the fountain was a pair of mosaic breasts coming out of the ground.

When the Journal caught up with De Soto Mayor, she was scrubbing the graffiti off and explained the breasts, 'Represented family and community.' She then said *screw you* by posing for a photo between two jets of water from its nipples.

Ethan ollied up over the fountain wall, landed on the B-side transition, and pumped across the multi-coloured surface. The Spawn album clipped the limits of his headphones, replacing the sound of children laughing, chirping birds, and leaves in the wind.

The fountain was only available to ride once a year when it was drained for cleaning. Today it buzzed with kids on their boards, trying to slash up to the lip and stick a grind worth sharing online. A few kids noticed Ethan and moved to the sides to watch. He hated that, but knew, like them, he had to seize the chance to ride.

During previous years, each attempt to ride resulted in a voodoo powered slam, collision, or near-death experience. He'd rather not be watched as the kids always expected to see him do something amazing—which was one of the downsides to having thousands of subscribers on Network 27's video channel. And as much as he hated being sponsored by N27, he just couldn't walk away from that paycheque, just yet.

When he started at the company, the biggest perk was the private health cover. His issues were the first appointment booked in praying for the hope for a *condition*.

'It's my ears,' he told the doctor.

He didn't have a clue what he was asking for, but the medicals were five-star rated, so why suffer. The doctor asked all the pre-test questions whilst stabbing a biro in the relevant check-boxes. In a dance around the obvious, Ethan decided not to mention it affected his riding: that would get him sacked, and; he also couldn't say the Fountain scared the life out of him: that was just weak. Instead, he chose to lead the doctor down a blind alley of complaints and hope for a suitable, albeit unlikely, diagnosis. A sympathy card would have been a blessing, a free pass, an excuse: *Shit, mate. I would, but I've got this ear-thing.*

No chance.

The kids watched as Ethan carved up to the lip and felt a clickity-click under his back truck. The pump down and back up again begged for something different. On any other transition his back truck would have dropped into a smith, but with nothing to lock into he slipped his wheels over into a lip-slide, held the slide until it almost stopped, then rocked the board back in again.

In the back of his mind, he couldn't shake off the slams of previous years. The Fountain had had a bite and knew Ethan's blood tasted great. Still, he couldn't resist squeezing his fat body of hope through a small window of opportunity.

Once again, he carved across the tiles to the opposite side of the Fountain. He could have tried a crook-grind, a tail-slide, or even a lip-slide, but no, he was determined to keep it simple.

It didn't matter.

Fate played its card anyway.

Just as he committed to a rock and roll slide, a kid in a bright yellow t-shirt rolled into his peripheral vision. Ethan held the slide for three seconds at full speed. His feet were good, the wall slid well, his weight was spot-on, but that kid was there, glowing like a ripe zit. Was the kid riding towards him? He couldn't tell. Was he stepping off his board or falling off?

It didn't matter. His concentration was lost.

On the way in from the rock, his front wheel caught on the lip which shifted his foot across the grip tape and landed heel heavy. As soon as his weight settled, his board shot to the right and slammed him into the floor. His shoulder took the hit, then his head, ribs, and hip.

A wheezy grunt of lung-dust stifled every swear word in his vocabulary as Marilyn Manson sang *Trip Like I Do* into his ears.

He was getting tired of this. Riding never used to be this random. Sometimes after a slam—even if it wasn't too bad—the floor felt safe and soft like a bed of embarrassment whilst his skin burnt with regret and hopeful sympathy. Welcome to the Fountain, again. *Damn water features.* Ethan rolled onto his back and saw a silhouette step into the light.

'You alright?' The voice was familiar.

'Yeah.' Ethan lifted his hand to his eyes. It was his mate, Ren.

'Shame.' Ren walked off again.

Ren hadn't been seen for months and though Ethan knew he'd run into him some time, he was beginning to believe he'd been ostracised completely.

'Hey, wait up.' Ethan rolled onto his side. 'I think I broke a rib.'

Ren looked back. 'You just slapped some fat.'

2

REN'S ARRIVAL

'Wait up.' Ethan caught up with him. 'You're not avoiding me, are you?'

The flash of a little white Emerica logo on Ren's shoes said *new*. Everything's always good with new shoes.

'Tss.' Ren's teeth whistled like a kettle. 'Same old Ethan.'

'You staying for a skate? It would be good to catch up.'

'I'm just leaving.' Ren slid his phone into his shorts.

'Why? Am I toxic?'

'Damn right you're toxic. Because of you, Chris is flipping burgers, Elliott is still out of work, and I'm delivering newspapers.'

Apologies always came slowly to Ethan. He believed Accidents involving friends shouldn't need

7

Apologies because it obviously wasn't intended—hence the friendship. Yet Ren believed a series of stupid decisions couldn't just be an Accident. The first one was *the* Accident. All other Accidents were just part of the clean-up process. Ethan always viewed Accidents as a whole—no matter how many there were. Even then, it appeared that acknowledgement wasn't the point either. People preferred Blame and Suffering. Blame and Suffering fixed everything. Oh, and Regret. People love that one too.

'C'mon, mate. We're—we were—friends. What have I got to do? I screwed up.'

Behind him, a small voice in a distracting yellow t-shirt said, 'Why, what did you do?'

'Yeah, tell him, E,' Ren said. 'Tell the kid what you did, exactly.'

The little kid's interruption slid up the smooth crack of Ethan's apology like a lemon-scented baby wipe. 'Because I did a bad thing. Hey, do you want to skate a pool? Super-local, just been discovered. I'm going there later.'

'Shut up and don't try and wriggle out of this. You tell him what you did.'

The pool was a way better distraction to be talking about, and though Ren wasn't much of a pool skater either, it was brand new.

He tried to tempt Ren for a session again and spilt more about what the Network had come up with. It was too good to miss, but Ren wasn't interested. He just wafted Ethan's excuses away and implied the little kid was still waiting. It was hard to think about how to start a story when every starting point appeared bad. Plus, he didn't know exactly how much Ren knew. He sure knew a lot but whether it was the truth, was another matter. Instead, Ethan did what he always did and played it down. 'I stole some stuff, and they lost their jobs,' he admitted.

'Nice try.' Ren's kettle was ready to blow judging by the whistle from his teeth. 'Here's what really happened. This idiot knew that his sponsor—who also sponsored his friends—had money trouble. We had this tour lined up which was make or break for the company. During the trip, he stole the tour van, blew the engine up, spent five thousand pounds at the garage, *and* paid for it using the money out of *our* bags once the company credit card hit its limit.'

'It was a mistake.' His defence had worn thin, but it was all he had. 'I thought the mechanics were fixing the engine, not replacing it with a brand new one!'

'There's more. Then he acted like a prick…'

The kid smiled at the swear word.

'… he smashed into a car.'

'That was a separate incident, and no-one regrets it more than me.'

A fresh booger came out of the kid's nose which he examined closely.

'The child lost its mother.'

The kid looked back at his dad on the library bench scrolling through his phone.

'Crippling his brother.'

'He's recovering well, though.'

'… and blaming him for the crash.' Ren paused. 'Everyone apart from the judge knew *you* were driving. Idiot.'

'People make mistakes.'

'But *you* make *all* of them in one day!' Ren drew a big circle in the air when he said *all*.

'We're cool now, though, right?' Ethan said.

Ren's teeth whistled once more as he dropped his board and skated off.

'What do you want me to do!?' Ethan shouted after him.

The kid held out a bag of sweets, 'Want one?'

'You know accidents happen, right?'

'One time,' the kid slurped saliva from his gums, 'I drowned my hamster.'

Ethan took a sweet and ate it. 'That's not the same.' A milli-second later his lips pursed, and his eyes stretched into a watery squint. 'Ergh.' He spat the sweet out. 'What the hell are those things?' The acid attack on his tongue wouldn't ease up, despite using his t-shirt to mop up the excess saliva in his mouth.

The kid threw another one into his spit hole. 'Crystallised ginger.'

N27's maintenance man, Eric, walked his stiff hips over from the bus stop. Eric was one of the few people who hadn't patronised Ethan for skateboarding. He didn't understand the appeal, but if you had to drill a spy-hole into the mind of his demographic, at least Eric's wouldn't narrow up and trickle sticky with opinions. Despite not being on the official email list, Eric knew all about the arrival of N27's new Managing Director, Michael Blacker, and his plans to spark some life into the schedule. Everyone knew he was brought in to overhaul the business, but Human Resources glittered it up by reminding everyone he'd just come from LBC who were up in profit, strong in market share, and killing it on the socials.

'Redundancies.' Eric put his shopping on the floor and left his smile there. Gossip and uncertainty had slapped the happy optimist out of him.

'Nah.' Ethan tried to crank that smile back up. 'We've gone through enough changes already. It'll be all good from here. Maybe some new opportunities?' As soon as he said the words, the distance between their jobs became clear.

'Opportunities, when you're my age,' Eric said, 'means retirement.'

A ride-on toy ambulance by the library door started up and an 8-bit electronic siren pierced the air. Eric winced and reached for his hearing aid. The child shrieked with joy; his little head rocked dangerously backwards and forwards, whilst his mother pulled a strand of hair from her mouth with a painted fingernail.

Ethan checked his emails, ignored the 1,938 unread ones, and searched for any company mail-outs. He found two from yesterday. The first, from the HR department, clarified Blacker's arrival with some historical background and asked everyone to give him a warm welcome. Trust HR to initiate the ass-kissing process with a carefully crafted email. He imagined a queue for the joy-burrito ready to fall out of Blacker's ass. The second email was from his boss.

'Flint doesn't sound happy,' Ethan said.

'She just needs a hug.'

'No, I mean she's telling me this deadline is important.'

'Do you think she's trying to impress the new MD?' Eric still had his finger in his ear.

'For sure,' Ethan said. 'Between you and me, I hope she doesn't make it to the end of the week.'

'Do you want to put a pound on that?' Eric took his keys out of his pocket and jangled them like he needed to be somewhere, as there was still about twenty-five-pence worth of siren to go. 'I saw that fall you just had. It looked painful.'

'I'm fine. I've got to skate a pool this week and thought I'd get some practice in.'

Eric looked perplexed until Ethan explained that a pool was a cross between a skatepark and a swimming pool, like the Fountain, but five times deeper.

'I hope you're wearing a helmet,' Eric chuckled.

'I've got my helmet here.' Ethan pointed to a scar on the side of his head.

Eric's bus pulled up at the stop. He gathered up his bags and said he'd see Ethan tomorrow. The old sod struggled with those hips and Ethan thought about all his past injuries. Sixty-year-old skaters throwing arthritis parties in their Care Homes. Shares in painkillers would be a good long-term investment. He gave his thigh another rub. Death threw a cloud of shade over the library and blew the word Loser around his ears, he knew the Fountain had got him again.

One day though. One day.

3

TV TROUBLE

Ethan slapped his hands down on the vinyl counter of SmartHome's Information Desk, pushed a stack of 1200% APR leaflets to one side, and spread his TV rental contract out.

The girl held up a little cosmetic mirror to save an eyelash with a fingernail and had a badge above her boob with the name *Shona* on it. Her slow look stunk of red wine, her back-combed hairdo throbbed with the scent of fag ash, and her evenings coughed with the peppery sweat of a burlesque dancer.

'It says here, that I agree to make payments of £71.50 a month for 24 months, and the final total is £1716. That's twice as much as the TV's worth.' Between them was a shatterproof window heavily scratched with customer enquiries.

'You've got great taste in electronic equipment.' Shona flicked chewing gum around her glossed lips.

'But my bank account says you're taking £106 a month, which makes it £2544.'

Her heavy mascara made her eyelids blink in slow motion like it was painful. 'Yes, we sent you a new contract which you agreed to.'

'I didn't receive anything. It was probably sent to my old address.'

'You've changed addresses?' A form appeared and was slid under the glass. 'You really should have told us, Mr Wares. This will incur an administration charge, which will need to be backdated. Sign and date and post it back to us.'

An employee called Philip brushed Shona's ass with his hand as he passed. She quivered and her face softened like turkey flesh falling off the bone at Christmas. The kiss she blew back was a lunchtime code for biscuits and blowjobs. Ethan clicked his fingers to get her attention.

'How much is that going to be? Actually, forget it, I don't want to know. I'm not paying.'

'Failure to pay will result in the TV being repossessed. The paperwork was sent to you on the 26th of May of last year.' It was impressive to watch a vacuous soul deliver their Terms and Conditions so eloquently.

'But I didn't reply.'

The script continued, 'Customers are automatically upgraded to the new payment plan for their convenience.' Philip fired an elastic band which hit her on the side boob. 'Ow!' A stapler hit the wall beside him.

'You're robbing me. How is that convenient?'

Shona activated a customer services mode even DARPA would be proud of. 'We take care of all the paperwork. I'm sorry if you're not happy with the process, but we don't make the rules, we're just a regional branch.'

'I want to make an official complaint'

A laminated form somehow appeared on the counter without losing a stroke from filing her nails. Ethan's biro slid across the glossy surface as if it had come from a joke shop. 'This one doesn't work,' he said.

The girl passed another pen under the glass shield.

'This one doesn't work either.'

'Phil!' She shouted out to the backroom. 'A customer needs help filling in a form.'

'I don't need help. I need a pen that works.'

Philip appeared beside him, 'Do you want me to do it for you?'

'Fuck off, Philip.'

Philip glanced at Shona, who glanced back at Ethan. 'We're not obliged to serve you if you continue using profanity.'

'Just give me a pen which works, then.' Ethan flung the biro across the counter.

'We're going to have to ask you to leave, Mr Warts.'

'I didn't swear.'

'You're being belligerent.'

Ethan snatched a black marker out of Philip's hand, signed and dated the form, then slid it back under the glass.

'You've got to post it,' she said.

'I'm here. Just take it.'

'It's got to go to head office,' Philip said.

Ethan felt a tap on his shoulder. 'You gunna be long mate?' A short man in a greasy mac and even greasier hair, stood with a carrier bag of DVDs. He inhaled like a Pug and exhaled like a Kazoo.

'Head office,' Philip said.

'Mate,' said the Pug.

'Post it,' Shona said.

'Head office.'

'Mate?'

'Post it.'

Ethan stretched out his hand as he walked through the electrical aisle and slapped every item on the shelf. Toasters tumbled, Hi-fi's twisted, and Juicers toppled. The security guard at the entrance was ready for him, however, all sixty-eight kilos of the minimum wage agency employee, couldn't stay upright as Ethan shoved the middle of his chest. The man clattered against the staff award photographs on the back wall and Ethan strode out into the High Street without looking back.

Head office, Mate, Post it.

4

MARKED MAN

A dent in the sign for the leisure centre looked like someone had taken a full swing at it with a bat. The vinyl letters had peeled away over the last thirty-years as if to endorse the public retreat from such a badly managed facility.

Despite the good afternoon light, it was still the colour of pigeon shit. In its more profitable times, the centre had offered a cricket pitch, tennis and netball courts, and high diving boards into a swimming pool with a head-crackingly shallow deep-end. Eventually, EU Health and Safety officers scrapped any sign of certification and insisted the diving boards be removed. They then went on to find an inadequate boiler system, a breach of virtually all known fire regulations, and an asbestos roof.

Ethan hadn't been inside before, but years ago friends had told him it resembled a landfill site.

Recently, new information had landed on the desk of the research team at N27 and the next thing he knew they wanted him in there to film a pool. He acted surprised and happy and should have celebrated with the joy of Ubley having some hidden talents, except he couldn't. It was a damn pool. Instead, a cloud of *fucks* sat over him ready to rain *sakes* for the rest of the week.

There was a new chain wrapped around the old gates to warn away strangers, however, being a card-carrying resident meant special privileges applied. There were plenty of other ways to get into the leisure centre, but Ethan's impetus took on a lazy pace lately as fate kept screwing with him. He called it his *Slings and Arrows of Outrageous Fortune.* Example: Seconds earlier, he'd thrown his board up over the fence and watched it fall into a hole in the ground. An idiot-bulb illuminated his brain as soon as it left his fingertips.

So instead of a short walk along a path less troubling, he was suffering his *Slings and Arrows.* It was hard to fathom whether the universe purposefully toyed with him or whether he created that life for himself. It would have been a joy to know that nothing he did made any difference. Fate, again, playing its card.

He jammed a foot into a gap in the gate and climbed over the top.

From a distance the leisure centre had a shape

of prominence and solid joyful memory, but up close, close enough to feel the texture of the cement, it lost that shape and took on a new one. When it was open, visitors projected their emotions and gave it a heart. Now, without all that joy, the place broke the blue sky into pieces, disorientated the wind, and left unwelcome surprises behind every corner. More of a happy abattoir.

One of the big old rooms had lost its door to thieves years ago and invited a look. The floor had absolutely no indication of its purpose, the ceiling, however, was perfectly intact. The room was the size of a tennis court, two floors high, and had a balcony on the left. Between the roof joists were acrylic banners of people in various states of play: running, swimming, laughing, hitting stuff. At ground level, everything had been trashed or robbed. 'Boo!' he shouted into the emptiness, and it ricocheted back. A scavenging pigeon rose from the floor and flew out through a broken window. Ethan explored some more rooms.

The shaft which swallowed his board ran along the main Lido building. It had a partially damaged roof which did little to shelter it from the elements. Though this was not the pool he was after. This pool was rectangular and now resembled a skip which only a JCB could clear. Professional fly-tippers had made it their home to avoid charges at the recycling centre. Over the decades more and more debris had been thrown in and now the fifty by twenty-five-metre pool needed a dozen trucks to empty it. According to Ethan's map, his pool was further out towards the sports fields, but without that board, he wouldn't be rolling anything.

After completing a lap around the edge of the pool, without finding any exits, he returned to the open plan main entrance surrounded by a cafe, gym, small halls, and changing rooms. Everything felt like it had been evacuated after a major emergency. A door to the left had been wrenched off its fittings and revealed the stairs for the next level down. A faded sign declared additional equipment bays, maintenance rooms, stores, laundry, and boilers meant for operational staff only.

At the bottom of the stairs, the darkness pressed on his chest. Despite little shafts of light offering a small route of visibility and oxygen, it didn't make him feel any better for it. If Light equals Hope, the absence of it means all Hope is Lost. Ethan always felt that life got blacker when it intended to screw with him.

Despite being dry outside, underneath the complex, drips of water echoed through the damp corridors. He kicked through old newspapers, tin cans, and pushed wooden crates out of his way. The plan was to get as close to the location of the board and figure out how to reach it from there.

On the door frame to one of the rooms,

someone had sprayed a dot of bright blue paint the size of a tennis ball with an arrow pointing left. It was only noticeable because he'd seen it a few times before. Always the same shape and colour, except the arrow pointed in different directions. It was too dull to be a graffiti tag and reminded him of buildings marked for demolition, or trees marked for felling.

The Keep Out sign on the front gate had a notice attached to it which he hadn't read. It could have been a notice from the council or a demolition warning.

Dynamite? he thought.

He paused and listened for any efficient professionals quietly tagging the rooms. Yet he only heard condensation drips and the wind brushing leaves against the windows outside. Once the last dregs of daylight disappeared behind him, he headed for a light leak from a gap in the window boarding on the back wall. He pressed his face up to the light and breathed for a moment. The daylight and fresh air felt cool and clean, unlike the mould spores he'd inhaled for the last ten minutes. As he resumed his search, he was sure the spot where his board fell was level with the next room, and it took a while for his eyes to adjust to the darkness again.

An oil can on the floor had been split open, the fluid left a wet patch, but there was still plenty more inside. He found a dirty rag and soaked up the rest of the residue, then lit the edge with his lighter. The flame crawled slowly across the cloth until the oxygen coaxed the flames into life and the heat brushed his eyebrows. He slid it onto a short piece of wood and walked it back into the room. Another blue dot on the doorframe again. Perhaps a locals-only marking for a safe route out? It was good to know that whoever put them up kept their friends in the loop.

As he went through the doorway, the light startled something. It was large, an animal, a deer, a fawn. The thing bounded around the room in a panic and pushed right into him on its way out. A second fawn bounced around in the same panic. This time he got away from the door, but something caught his foot and tripped him. He dropped the flame to save himself but landed face down in some netting. In the struggle to get free, he twisted around but tangled himself more and more in the process. He couldn't stand or reach the floor and the harder he pulled the more he realised he was trapped.

5

———

THRASHIN'

The netting consisted of hundreds of lines of fishing wire loosely draped over and under each other across the pit. The burning oil flame on the floor flicked light against the wall and released a plume of black smoke up to the ceiling. This was bad. He was stuck and he knew it. He wanted to call for a friend until he remembered he was alone. Riding by himself was one thing, but to be in trouble was something else. If Ren was there, they would have laughed their heads off. Ren would've wound him up and took photos for sharing later before eventually heaving him out.

On the plus side, the smoke might work like gossip on the conscience of a passer-by before it choked him out completely. The taste of the air changed, tanged his throat, and stuck to his mouth. He spat a few times. The metal oil can crackled under the pressure of the heat. All he needed was some steaks frying next to him and this barbecue party would be ready. Some guests would be nice.

He shouldn't have gone in the building alone. Maybe Ren would've come along if asked. He thought he did, but then maybe he didn't. Either way, it was stupid not to try.

Those *Slings and Arrows.*

He and Ren would've cleared up their misunderstandings from the past in an hour, tops. Equal distribution and they'd be rolling like kings once again. Sure, Dixel was a friend too, but not like Ren was. The number of trips they'd been on, before being sponsored, growing up, and learning to skate. All that blown away.

He tried again to get free of the fishing line by kicking and pulling his feet and heaving hard on the ones around his hands. *Just pull harder, I can get this.* It only made things worse. Another approach was needed. He twisted around to his right and tried to pull his hand through a loop to give it a little more freedom. Once he did, he dropped his shoulder and pulled his elbow back until it unhooked itself. All that freedom came with a downside: listing to the right. It might as well have been cheese wire pressing on his limbs of fresh Brie.

The flicker of light dancing against the wall was calming at least, and that fawn was so beautiful, light-footed, and young. He wished it returned to see what all the fuss was about.

It was at that moment, he thought of the solid padlock on the gate, and how no-one came through the complex to even visit. If he screamed for help, no-one would hear him.

Screaming for help: go figure.

His five-year-old self learnt to stop screaming for help when nightmares hung around after he'd woken. A few years later the seal in his bedtime bladder would burst a stain of shame all over his future like a beacon of rejection.

Still, with the predicament at hand, that shame edged closer to a cliff-edge.

Nervous laughter did little to ease the cut and pinch on his leg. Some blood flow down there would be nice, what with it all mainlining through to his sweat sensors. Occasionally, a car would pass by on the road and ghost-walk leaves around. Little comfort Hope was teasing him like that. With the cliff edge in sight, a quiet apology to Ren formed which got easier with practice and gave Elliott and Chris a moment too. Once the simple toast to absent friends faded, he remembered the lighter in his jacket pocket.

Could he reach it?

After twisting back on himself to straighten up, he pulled his stretched hand closer to his chest. The zip on his jacket sleeve got caught on another wire and prevented him from turning any nearer. He couldn't unhook it but managed to get a fingertip to the fabric, pick the edge open, and reach inside.

A one-inch flame blinked into life and lit up the web of wires. Whoever created that trap built a lid of wires to flip shut on the prey as well ensuring it wouldn't get out. However, they didn't account for opposable thumbs and a zippo. The lighter melted away the plastic threads around his hand with such ease he felt sympathetic towards all that effort to build it. The web of lines illuminated around him became a joy to ignite and watch as it recoiled. Stupid trap. Once everything was clear around his hand, he needed to twist around and unhook his elbow. The new position meant he could reach down his right side to his feet. Sixty-seconds tops, he bet himself, so sure with confidence. But all that joy just clogged up his concentration. Focus gave way and he paid for it. He massaged the lighter around in his hand for a better position and lost his grip. The lighter bounced off the side of his thumb, the flame cut out, and despite trying to catch it in the dark, it pin-balled off the wires and landed on the floor.

'Fuck!'

Patience is a virtue not found in this hole of regrets. Patience is for people who have got their shit together. That lid of wires was a cold call. Callous, you could say. What beast would get joy from this? His stomach knot clamped enough to challenge his bladder gasket for the first time in years. His sweat to heart-rate ratio overlapped enough to turn a Venn diagram into a full circle. The math pressed hard on his decisions—clearing his throat helped—and a surprising moment of calm tickled him.

In the silence of the moments that passed, an observer would question the prey, and suppose it had resigned to its fate or exhausted itself to rest. Yet, this fleshy lump just flipped a coin of fucks hoping for the sunny side to land face up. How long before that oily rag burnt through, throwing him in to complete darkness for hours, all night, and maybe for days? No-one would know but the deer that might return if it could stomach the stench of piss and sorrow. Eventually, that tickle edged up from his belly, crawled through his burnt stench dry throat, and trickled out as a whimper.

'Help?' He asked the universe.

This was just a self-conscious test of the acoustics; nothing more than a mic check. What he needed was some intention, he had the impetus, but lacked effort.

'HELLO?!'

A few embarrassing seconds of pause was needed to listen for something: Thumper, Bambi, or Wil'o the damn Wisp. He imagined someone standing outside the window at the bus stop who thought, *was that a cry for help?* and dismissing it as it didn't sound panicky enough. He thought about all the car alarms he'd heard in the night that he hadn't reacted to, assuming it was a false alarm. Society was doomed if distress needed a plausibility review. So, after he'd punched his pride out of existence, the next shout came at maximum volume and stretched until his lungs ran out of oxygen.

'HELLLL-P!'

The strain in his throat cracked his voice like a twelve-year-olds. It was a scream so embarrassing he wished no-one heard it, but somebody did.

A crate moved from deep within the darkness of the other room. One of the same crates that he had almost fallen over on the way in. Every inch of him didn't want to shout again, but this was a ship on the horizon he just had to wave at.

'Hello! Is anyone there?'

After a moment of rustling footsteps through the papers, he tried again.

'Can you help me? I'm stuck. Hello?'

It could have been Dixel, but she would have responded, so he hoped it wasn't anyone he knew. There's nothing worse than being rescued by a familiar face. Another rigid thrust and twist on those wires just sliced his cheese further until he noticed the figure of a man in camouflage clothes in the doorway.

'I'm...' Obviously, he was stuck. D'uh. 'Can you help?'

The man considered his options before moving forward, 'What are you doing here?' he said.

In such a heightened situation, just one-hundredth of a second's hesitation raised enough internal alarms to open a cowbell franchise. Something could have been done by now. *Oh, no. Of course, I'll help. One moment.* Instead, this fool stood there as if seriously considering whether Ethan was worth the effort to squat. As if he had better things to do. That hesitation space played its tricks and before he knew it he was smiling, pitiful, shameful, and full of nervous hope that the man wouldn't just walk away.

'You shouldn't be here,' the man said.

So what? Just get me out of here! 'I know. I know.'

The man made his decision and pulled out a large hunting knife, crouched, and sliced along the fishing line from top to bottom. Ethan dropped to the floor and pulled the tangled wires from his limbs.

The man had already left the room. 'Get out of here,' the darkness told him.

'Hey, wait!' He climbed out of the pit, and stumbled to catch up through the rooms, to the stairs, and out into the daylight.

They cut across the shabby grass of the recreation ground towards a small caravan on the horizon. The hunting knife strapped to the man's thigh sat above the pocket of his combats; out of the other pocket stuck the blue lid of a spray can. His right hand gripped the front legs of a dead fawn. It dripped spots of red on the ground and its ears bounced in a cute way when the man's boots occasionally kicked it. At just a few paces behind him, Ethan made sure to scuff his feet to let the man know he was still close. 'Thanks for cutting me loose back there.' Bluebottles homed in on the dead animal but struggled to choose between it and Ethan. 'Do you work here?' He added. 'I mean, like, look after the place?' An unwashed scent of homelessness clung to the man's clothing like a force field; knuckles like sandpaper; fingernails clipped tight like his chat. 'So, I was wondering if you could help me out? I'm looking for…'

'The exit is that way,' the man nodded towards the fence.

'Thanks, but I'm actually after an old pool.'

Ethan told him that he worked for the Network 27 and if the man had watched much TV on a Saturday morning, he may have seen some skateboarding. That would have been him.

'I don't see a skateboard,' the man said.

The damn thing was still in the drain. 'I've lost it. I was trying to find it.'

The closer they got to the caravan the more it lost its cute appeal. A smooth gradient of grime from the bottom met with a gradient of mould from the top to the point where the white band in the middle closed up like the final chapter in its life. The tires: flat; its wheels: jacked up on bricks; the cracked plastic window had been taped up, and nothing says *Home Sweet Home* like a footprint in your front door. The man dropped the deer on the ground, slid his knife blade up the door seam to unlock it, entered, and slammed the door behind him.

Well, that was some bullshit.

The leisure centre looked a good four-hundred metres away; a housing estate to the far left, separated by a thick hedgerow; to the right, a chain-link fence ran the rest of the perimeter, with just fields beyond that. A crow glided overhead which he aimed at with gun fingers and shot out of the sky. Behind the caravan was a familiar rounded edge of a slab of pale concrete, attached to another, and another. It was pool coping.

6

——————

HITTING THE OLD BOAT

Just a few feet from the far side of the caravan, a pool laid hidden like a jewel in this otherwise decrepit shithole. It had steps at the shallow end and went to about nine feet in the deep. The coping had been ridden, but not much. How could no-one have spotted it? Ethan jumped down for a closer look.

'This is mental!' He couldn't hide his smile.

He walked down the length of the pool and as the horizon disappeared the sound changed. He couldn't hear the grass rustling, the finches twittering around the shrubs, the traffic from the road, or the breeze brushing against the smallest hairs in his ears. It was a warm, silent sun trap. If only he had his board. The caravan was almost completely out of sight from the deep end and the coping looked super intimidating.

The pool was the dogs and about as far away from the Library Fountain as you could get. When he accepted this location, two things shot through his mind: *How the hell can I film this? And don't tell them I can't skate pools.* Working out everything on the fly was something every skateboarder was used to, so he vowed to worry about it later. Before he arrived, a bunch of Figures slammed into his forehead: he figured Research screwed up; he figured the pool wouldn't have transitions; he also figured it would most likely suck so bad it would be unrideable. However, he didn't figure that he'd be wrong on all counts. Making a convincing edit which wouldn't die in the ratings or embarrass him, wouldn't be easy. He wouldn't be able to fake pool skating. Plan B began to float through all his figuring. This was a special location which would benefit from some friends.

'Get out of there!' A voice said from behind. The man stood on the coping at the shallow end with a baseball bat beside his leg.

'You knew about this? I mean, of course, you did. This is what I've been looking for. I'm supposed to be riding this.'

'You're trespassing.'

'What? You're going to kick me out?' Ethan thought quickly. 'You don't work here. What kind of groundsman lays traps and kills deer? I want to see some ID.'

'And you're not a skateboarder,' the man said. 'You'd have your board if you were going to ride.'

'I told you I lost it. If I had my board, I'd shred this thing.'

'Wait there.' The man took a step back and returned to his caravan.

The guy was a joke, waving around a baseball bat like that. It's one thing to carry a weapon and something else to use it. He had seen fools like this plenty of times before and it was always easy to taunt, tease, and distance himself from the crazies. This guy had Slow written all over him and it wouldn't be hard to get out of the pool and leg it across the field.

It turned out N27 was right about the spot, however they'd been slack to put details together. Usually, he'd get a full report on the location, but this time he hadn't, for some reason. They seemed to just punt him in the right direction and let him get on with it. Maybe Heston knew and realised the find would be a bad-assed surprise. It was such a gem. If only he could ride it.

When the man returned, he threw a skateboard into the pool.

'Here you go. Prove it,' he said.

The board was something out of the eighties: flat, wide, and covered in plastic. The griptape had that well-worn shine to it, the type that couldn't damage your shoes even if you hated them. The underside had been stripped of its graphic and replaced with a collage of stickers, a US dollar bill, and some stencilled lettering, then all honey glazed with a thick golden varnish. Black rails matched the trucks and it had soft pitted wheels with rusted bearings. The accessories kept coming: a black nose-bone, lapper, and a small tail-block bulged its profile. It was only good for the skip.

'I can't skate this.'

'Of course, you can't.'

'No, I can't skate *this*. Don't you have anything from this decade?'

'You said you're famous around these parts. You said I might have heard of you. So, prove it Mr Big-shot.'

'I'll level with you…'

'Skate or leave. I don't have time for this,' the man tapped his baseball bat against his leg.

'Jesus.' Ethan got on the board. 'Just give me a moment to get the feel of this boat.'

The man sat on an old camping chair. 'I can wait.'

Ethan pushed off into the deep end and immediately felt the stiffness of the bearings. With a second harder push he pumped about halfway up the transition, and almost lost it on the kick turn. That flat tail sucked. The pump back down didn't give him enough speed to get back up to the shallow end. After taking a tight turn he pushed back down into the deep. The bearings freed up a little more and he got right up underneath the coping. The pump back down was also better, but if the plan was to impress the man, a few kick turns weren't going to achieve anything. Though for sure the man wouldn't have a clue what a trick was, so as long as he didn't fall off, he could pretty much do anything and impress him. On the third push into the deep end, he had enough speed to slash a smith on the coping. The back truck locked into the grind and despite leaning into it, the angle was all wrong. The board stopped dead, but he managed to unlock it before being pulled back in. The vert caught him out, as his weightlessness shifted his front foot across the griptape and caused him to run out on the flat.

'Is that all you've got,' said the man.

'No.' It felt like riding the Great Wall of China. 'I'm just getting started.' He went up for a rock-to-fakie and pushed the deck a little on the coping to see if it slid on those stupid rails. As with all things plastic, the rails sucked, but he figured the slip would be the same as riding plastic gas pipes. After successfully rolling to fakie, he pushed again and got up into a fifty-fifty, but the board stuck again, and he ran out. The man laughed at his weak effort.

'I told you I could ride.'

'That's not riding.' The man sniffed. 'You've just proved you *can't* ride.'

'If I had my board...'

'Don't blame the equipment.' The man got out of his seat and went back to the caravan. 'Get off my property.'

He didn't own that place, he was just another gatekeeper with issues. If the man flipped out, Ethan knew he could dodge that bat, but he wanted his board back. The thought of walking around the leisure centre in the dark again, with hell-knows how many traps that moron had set, didn't thrill him.

'Ok, look, I agree, I'm crap at this, but can you help me get my board back? Then, I'll leave,' he lied.

'And you can't get it because?' the man shouted from inside the caravan. Ethan got out of the shallow end and walked to the front door. Those hinges barely held it in place. He didn't know this man from Adam and for that reason only he didn't care what he thought. He'd already cried like a baby in that pit, it's not like opening up a little more was going to destroy their friendship.

'I don't. Like. Being in there.' The words dropped on the floor like squash balls. When there was no reply, he gave it another go. 'I mean. I'm. Like. Phobic.' The man looked out of the window for a moment and disappeared again. 'I just struggle with things like that. Spaces.' The man was really making him spill his guts. 'If you know the area well, then I bet you could walk straight up to my board and get it. Please?'

The man came out into the doorway with a rag in one hand and an old car part in the other. 'You should speak to someone about that.'

'About what?'

'Your head.'

The man handed him a business card which said, *Loretta Deane, BA, MA, UKCP, Reg Psychotherapist.*

7

COUNCIL COLLISION

Ethan looked at the card, whilst the man walked back across the grass to the leisure centre. He didn't need a psychotherapist; he needed a pill; something to set his stomach straight. Loretta Deane probably charged a hundred pounds an hour to sit and watch the clock tick by. He saw a programme on phobia's once where a woman was frightened of spiders. Her cure? More spiders. What would they do for him? Lock him in a cupboard for a few days? He'd rather save the hundred and avoid the cupboard completely. That's the thing about *Treatments*, they're all bundled up with over-comings. If you weren't working to *Overcome* something, you were running *Away* from it. Avoidance therapy would be better. Still, instead of flinging the card across the dirt, he slid it into his pocket to bin later.

Just as he considered getting back in the pool,

an animal whimpered nearby. It sounded like a cat meow or possibly a fox. The chances of one of the bushes around him holding a den were high. It made sense that creatures stayed shush when the glint of a hunting knife threatened. Still, he couldn't see any fur balls tumbling loose from the nest or fighting for a spot on the teats.

Ethan pumped up into an axle stall, then kick-turned back to the shallow and hit another weak carve. The line back into the deep got him right up under the coping, but he lost his balance which forced him to bail.

Those bearings were the problem, and as long as the damn things turned, Reed probably wouldn't bin the setup. Logic stated: once they wouldn't spin —it'll be time for a burial. He spat into each of the shields to lube them up temporarily, but the skate didn't feel much better.

Still, even without his board, just for a small moment, it felt like being in the backyard of a vacant property in the Hollywood Hills. A complete sun- and sound-trap, except for the crunch of those pitted wheels broken by British pavements. The freedom was fantastic until a small stone caught his wheel, which skidded and sent him stumbling to the floor.

He picked himself up and threw the board and all its crap wood and plastic glory to the other end of the pool. Once it had finished clattering down the transition, he heard a small vehicle hum across the dirt.

It pulled to a stop and a Council branded car door creaked open. The bent frame of a fifties woman wrapped in a cat-lady cardigan huffed out of the driver's seat to the delight of the shock absorbers. She locked the car, for some reason, and looked surprised when Ethan stuck his head out of the pool. 'Oh, hello,' she said.

'If you're after the guy who lives there: he's not in.'

Her smile broke. 'Do you know where he is?'

'No.'

'You saw him leave, though?'

Jesus. She laid that question like a tripwire.

'Kinda.'

She repaired her smile and crouched at the pool's edge. 'My name's Kirsty Sapsford. I'm with the council.' A pendant swung forward from a chain at cleavage height and the hypnotist turned magician when a business card materialised out of thin air.

Ethan reached into his back pocket and pulled out his card. 'Ethan Wares: Skateboarder.' The Therapist's business card confused her. 'I don't actually have any cards.'

'It's ok.' She flipped the card over. 'So? …'

'Yep.' He accepted it back. 'It's for a friend.'

She turned her attention back to the caravan. 'Do you know Joel?' she said.

'Joel?'

'Joel Reed. The man who lives here?'

'Oh right, Reedy. Yeah. No. Not really. I just met him about twenty minutes ago. He'll be back shortly as he's just gone to...' The leisure centre looked too far away to be relevant. 'It doesn't matter. He'll be back in a bit.'

She stood up and looked over the pool. 'This looks fantastic. Have you been riding it?' She ran her finger over a map of the area. 'It doesn't appear to be on the plans.'

Ethan took out his map and mimicked her. 'You're right. I don't have it here either.'

'You have plans too?' There were two rectangular boxes together in the spot where they stood. It wasn't Reed's caravan, it was the wrong shape and size.

'Are those shipping containers?' he asked. Their heavy grass-compressed footprints were now clearly visible on the ground. 'How long do you think they've been there?'

'Our archives only go back ten years, as that's when the council took ownership.'

That didn't compute. The pool must have been there way before that as the locals would have discovered it. The thing would have had mythological status amongst the skaters. There was no way a decade could pass without someone finding it.

'I think it's been covered a lot longer than that,' Ethan said. 'It's pretty rare to even have one of these in the UK.'

'We'll have to update our records.' She placed a question mark on the map with a silver biro.

That wasn't good. Anything which involved updating records never ended well. It would be discussed in a meeting, assigned to a team member, risk-assessed, and someone, probably outside the council would be told to deal with it. Ethan knew the clock had started ticking. Time ticked for Kirsty too—for a coffee and cake in a lay-by somewhere.

'What's going to happen to this? Am I going to be able to skate it?' He knew he sounded like a spoilt child at Christmas, but instinctively he thought of the locals as well. His old crew might even speak to him again after this.

'Probably nothing will happen for months.' She cupped her hands to the window to see inside the caravan. 'But this is private land, so you shouldn't be here anyway.'

The part about nothing happening for months worried him. Months weren't very long for skateboarders who measured progress in years. A month is about a week. Worry ran along his skin ripping hairs from his forearms.

'What do you want with Reed?'

'To make sure he's looking after himself. We usually meet every month, but summer got in the way, so this is our first meeting since July.'

There was no sign of Reed on the horizon. 'The door's open,' Ethan said. 'He didn't lock it when he left.'

Kirsty pulled the door ajar a little. 'I'll just do a quick sweep.'

When you walk into a home you expect the scent of washing powder, cooked bacon, coffee beans, or laundry drying on a radiator. Instead, one sniff of the air tasted of damp mud and armpits. Ethan coughed into his hands another breath caught the smell of burnt toast. Military equipment was everywhere: boots, a jacket, belts, bags, maps, and ropes. All laid out neat and clean on a table and bench. A map of the world on the wall had overseas locations marked on it with a marker: Peru, the Middle East, and several places in Scandinavia. On the kitchen counter was the old car part Reed had been cleaning.

'He fixes and resells them.' Kirsty checked the fridge and sniffed a carton of milk. 'I've tried to get him to put them on E-bay, but I can't even get him to go to the library let alone use the Internet.'

A carrier bag on a chair contained reels of 0.26mm fishing line, 'I've already noticed he's good with his hands,' Ethan said.

Suddenly an animal whimpered from the back

room. They looked at each other as if to ask *Did you hear that?* On the floor of the bedroom was a large basket with eight Labrador puppies inside, yelping and jumping up for attention. Kirsty picked up a chocolate brown one. 'Hey there you.' She nuzzled its ear in return for a face lick. 'They must be just a few weeks old.'

Kirsty put one into his arms before he had a chance to refuse.

'I don't really like dogs.' It wriggled, yelped, nuzzled up for a licky-kiss, and then tried to nibble on his finger. He put the dog back before it could try anything else.

'They're adorable,' Kirsty said. 'And where's the mother? Did you see him leave with it?'

It figured that a hunter would need a dog at his side to do whatever hunting dogs do, but Reed didn't have one. A shadow passed by the dirty bedroom window.

'You can ask him yourself. He's back.'

The caravan listed slightly as Reed stepped into the doorway and seemed to glow with thousand fires. 'Put the dogs down and get out!' Ethan's board was thrown out on the dirt. Reed took the pup from Kirsty as she huffed on past him justifying her presence. She reassured Ethan with a shrug and a head shake that she'd experienced this reaction before. She seamlessly slipped into a calm conversation about rehousing, whilst he had a completely separate and much louder conversation about privacy, property, and personal space.

Ethan left them to it and jumped into the pool. Yet every time he skated up around the shallow end, he overheard them.

One instance of Kirsty's pièce de résistance appeared to be, '… let alone someone….'

Like him. Ethan finished the sentence in his head. Hopefully, she'd yanked the handbrake on that quip as anyone could see he had a military background. Even with all that ice in the air, her mouth couldn't stop in time.

'We have found a new flat for you.' She showed him the leaflet. 'It's perfect. You'll have all your bills paid for, we'll help with the transition, and it's available now.'

It felt like she'd rubber-stamped *Approved* on it, however, the leaflet only sat in Reed's hand long enough to scrunch it into a ball. He wasn't going anywhere. Kirsty got back in her car and said she'd come back again next week. Reed cussed her a few times and went back inside the caravan.

'Thanks for my board!' Ethan shouted. The miserable exchange hadn't put him off, it made him warm to the man a little more.

With his own board underfoot the pool felt less intimidating. The pump felt better and confidence grew with each kick-turn despite staying away from the coping. It was important that he took it easy, otherwise, he knew it'd spit him to the floor. The more comfortable he got, the higher he went until his lack of experience started to show. That coping looked worse at speed than it did with the slow boat underneath him. Zipping around in a dodgy figure-of-eight was harder than it looked. The hip seemed to appear out of no-where and disappeared faster than he'd like. Rock-fakies were completely useless in a pool which demanded carving, and ollie grabs were about a decade or two in the wrong direction. Inevitably though, the pool would get bored and slap him back to the floor whenever it felt like it. After one of many slams, Ethan laid out on his back and watched the clouds pass until the pain subsided.

'Mr Big-shot, you said.' Reed appeared at the coping and took a sip from a green camping mug. 'You can't even do the basics.'

He got to his feet and flipped the bird at the coping. 'This isn't skateboarding. There's a reason why people don't ride these things any more.'

Reed walked around to the deep end. 'Why's that?'

'These things went out with the 80's. And that board you gave me is a prime example: flat as a pancake and covered in plastic.'

'Spoken like a true has-been.'

Ethan chucked his board out onto the dirt and climbed out. 'I don't even know why I'm supposed to be riding this. No-one is going to watch it.'

'Not the way you ride.'

'Tss.' Ethan dug a stick into an ants nest and stirred it up. 'It ain't even worth the effort.'

'Any time you want to leave, go ahead,' Reed said.

The ants panicked and went into attack mode.

'Let's see you do it if you think it's so easy.'

'I thought you'd never ask.' Reed got up and went back into the caravan.

The ants climbed the stick, probably following a scent, or a hive-mind protocol, not that Ethan noticed. He was more focused on how the hell he could film a part. It took a few seconds to realise what the orange and yellow dots were scurrying over his fingers until they began to bite. He jumped up and slapped the back of his hand all over his leg.

'You're going to need some washing up liquid in those bearings, by the way.'

'Won't be needing any,' Reed shouted back.

When he came back out of the caravan he looked a different man. Gone were the stinking camouflage hunting clothes and replaced by shorts, pads, and an old helmet. Also, he had a different board. It was still old, but this one was clean and well kept. He sure looked every part the skater, just not from this decade.

'Blue and yellow Rectors?' Ethan said.

Reed stuffed some hip padding into the top of his shorts. He was a rider, alright, but how good, was yet to be proven. Plenty of old guys had turned up at the local park in the past and slalomed their way through a session like Turning was a trick. He got into the shallow end, slid an elbow pad up into position and pushed off into the deep. There was no stumble or wobble—just the opposite. He carved up into a frontside smith, pumped back up the other side and smacked his front wheels so hard into a Rock and Roll that the dirt bounced into the air. The rollout took him back up to the shallow end at full speed, he carved over the steps and rushed back down into the deep once more. A backside Rock and Roll slid across four or five blocks of coping. On the way back up the shallow, he went frontside back over the steps. It was easy and effortless. He finished off his run with an Invert and rolled to a stop in the shallow.

'I guess you're right,' he said. 'All that 80s crap is dead.'

8

———

LCPL JOEL REED

'I take it back. Where did you learn to skate like that?'

'Twenty years ago. But I'm no longer cool according to you.'

That Invert was textbook: extended and stalled, like a front cover. What he'd give for something like that. They were as elusive as layback grinds: a trick that should be easy but wasn't. Ethan just couldn't get into that squat position. An Invert, however, he didn't even know where to start. The last time he went upside-down he was being thrown up the stairs as a kid by his drunk dad. 'You've got to teach me those,' he said. 'That's the holy grail, right there.'

'I could, but,' Reed set his board down on his bag and slid his elbow pads off like he was done

57

already, 'you'd have to get past your attitude first. Do you like taking instructions?'

'Love it!' Ethan knew what Reed meant. He'd heard it plenty of times before. He didn't earn the nickname *Ethan Flares* for no reason. Reed needed a little more convincing. 'I'm supposed to pull an edit out of my ass here and you've seen me: I can't ride this thing. It's too…'

'Gnarly?'

'People don't say gnarly anymore. It's too bowl-y.'

Reed took his gear back inside the van and Ethan followed. The dogs heard the movement and began their demands for attention, and they only quietened once Reed poured some dry food into a bowl for them. After the initial shock of seeing the inside of the caravan, Ethan now saw it differently. This wasn't a space for someone out of control like Kirsty believed. His skating proved he was the opposite. Sure, the van was a mess, but it wasn't a lazy mess. It was a choice. The man had priorities and cleaning up wasn't one of them. Ethan pushed some papers over on the bench and sat, then immediately felt the wooden framework underneath the thin foam. A decorative wooden trim which ran the length of the wall distanced itself from the buckling surface, and the shelves bowed with years of damp. He hit the switch of a lamp on the sideboard and watched the bulb's filament wobble with Reed's footsteps at the other end of the van. When he returned from the back room, he laid the young deer out on a plastic sheet on the floor.

'You're an animal man, I can tell,' Ethan said. 'If you're not killing them, you're caring for them.'

'A man's got to eat.'

'Can't you just order a takeaway?'

'I could.' Reed swept the kitchen counter with a damp cloth. 'But I like to know where my food came from.'

Reed took his knife to the carcass and quickly slid the blade around all the fleshy parts. Peeling back the skin made Ethan wince. Talk about skinning up. Pretty barbaric for a living room. As much as he wanted to look out of the window or stare at the tins of food in the cupboard, he couldn't stop checking on Reed's progress. The man lived like a hobo on a budget of zero, last took a bath when the river was above ten degrees and was a target for Samaritan handouts. No-one would believe he chose the finest organic venison cuts for dinner. It only took a couple of minutes before he pulled the entire skin off the hoofs, and left the slippery carcass on the sheet. He placed the hide on the kitchen drainer, wrapped the deer in the sheet, and dropped it into a chest freezer behind the caravan. Then he laid the skin out on the kitchen counter and poured salt all over the inside to preserve it.

Flies arrived on a jet stream of foul air, but Reed's hands worked too fast for them to settle.

Ethan moved to the other side of the room in search of a more fragrant distraction. He found a notebook on the sideboard full of diagrams of grids, levers, and pulleys with arrows indicating directions. Each diagram had a name above it: *Spinner*, *Dropkick*, *Double-gate*, *worm-hole*, *rotor blade*, *scissors*. 'Hey, what's this?' he asked.

Reed glanced and continued rubbing salt into the hide. 'Those are traps.'

One diagram had a symbol he'd seen before with the name, *Tangle*. 'I was caught up in that?'

'And you wasted a lot of work and fishing line.'

'How many of these things are in there?'

'Twenty or so,' Reed said. 'All the walls are marked, so I don't forget. The last thing I want is for you to end up like Bambi here.'

That skin resembled nothing of the animal which barged past him in the leisure centre. The lump in the freezer was the real animal. The hide was just its two-dimensional identity. It reminded him of the front people put on, who wore half-truths like tattoos, uttered meaningless priorities, and slid ulterior motives into their actions. His ex, Amy, had her front of satisfaction, whilst planning to leave him. Also Flint, who wore her company front with *her* priorities, with *her* face, which she peeled off at the end of the day before falling asleep in her freezer.

'How long have you been living here?' Ethan asked.

'Since the summer…'

'That's not too bad.'

'… of 2008.'

A couple of million neurons fired until the Math arrived. 'That's. Quite. A while.' No wonder the caravan looked like it was on its last decade. 'The woman from the council seemed concerned about you staying here during the winter.'

'That doesn't bother me. I've done a stint in the Arctic circle.'

'That figures.' The uniform in the room stated the obvious. 'Why'd she mention it then?'

'She's new. She'll figure it out eventually.' Reed picked up the skin and brushed the loose salt off into the sink.

'Don't you want a free home?' Ethan noticed a couple of metal tags on the table. 'That must be hard to turn down. She seemed to think it was all sorted.'

'Not until I sign the papers, it isn't. I don't want it and she doesn't want to hear no.'

The tags must have been from Reed's troop. A five-digit number stamped into the surface looked like something he'd seen in a film. 'So, why are you staying here? There must be loads of other, more comfortable, places you could stay.'

Reed sighed. 'My section: Dan, Finley, Herman, Cameron, Ant, & Spencer, were based here, and they've gone off on a tour, and when they're done, they'll be back.'

'But it's been ten years.' Ethan flipped the tags over and over in his fingers. Reed carried a large sheet of board from the backroom to the kitchen and placed it against the wall. 'You think they've forgotten you, or maybe something went wrong?'

Reed didn't even look up. 'No.' He hooked the skin on a nail and began pinning it to the board with a small hammer. 'They've haven't forgotten.'

'You haven't heard anything? Have you tried to find them?'

'They don't want to be found. That'll be the last thing they'd want.'

Reed stretched the skin out. 'You any good with a hammer?'

Together they pinned the skin, with Ethan on the tools whilst Reed stretched the hide taut. Then Reed carried it outside to dry. Ethan quickly photographed the tags. He knew that Reed was waiting around for nothing. Ten years wasn't a tour, and it wasn't being AWOL either. People don't go away for that long without home contact. People get hurt, news travels, word gets around, if no-one is forgotten as Reed says, and no-one has contacted him in a decade, then they weren't going to. Ethan had an idea: if he could find out what happened to Reed's troop, maybe he would agree to teach him how to ride the pool.

A yelp from the puppies came from the bedroom and Reed went to pay them some attention.

'What's their story?' Ethan asked.

'I found them just a week ago in the main building.' Reed picked up a golden one and stroked it. 'They were abandoned.'

There was something rank in the room and it wasn't from the dogs. On the other side of the bed was a large bag full of knee pads, elbow pads, and helmets.

'These things need a wash, or they'll walk out of here on their own one day. Look at this thing.' He picked up a helmet. 'Who the hell would wear this?'

'I would.' Reed took the helmet from him and threw it back in the bag. 'It's a Flyaway helmet. Feel free to leave anytime you want.'

'I think we got off on the wrong foot. I'm sorry for disrespecting pool skating. And you're right, I don't like it because I can't ride it. But,' Ethan paused to let the penny drop, and when it didn't, he continued, 'if you could show me how to ride that thing, then...' He had nothing to offer Reed but hoped the blatant begging appealed.

Reed pondered the thought whilst messing with the puppy.

'It's not like you've got many choices really.' As soon as Ethan spoke, he regretted it, but the words kept tumbling out of his mouth. 'I know the pool is here now. I'm definitely coming back to ride it and I'm sure you don't want more people here shining a spotlight on your patch.'

'Are you threatening me?'

'No.' He hadn't even considered that, but Reed didn't look too pleased with being given an ultimatum. 'But you've got to admit that this place isn't going to remain a secret for long.'

Reed sighed to himself, put the puppy back in the basket, weighed up the time/cost ratio of *one cheeky bastard,* plus *could he be bothered* divided by *does he need this hassle.* As equations go, this was a dead cert. Eventually, Reed spoke with slow thoughts of regret. 'Ok. Tomorrow. Ten in the morning. And bring your pads.'

'Uh. I don't need any pads, and also, I don't have any.'

Reed picked up the stinking bag of pads and put them on the bed. 'I've got plenty you can borrow.'

'You've got to be kidding? Can you at least wash a pair?'

9

POOL LESSON

The second day at the leisure centre began with a kick out of bed. Heston had news for his brother. He and his girlfriend were officially getting together, which meant Ethan's sofa surfing had to come to an end. Despite having no-where to go, it was time to *pull his finger out*. Heston agreed to help him look for a new place, but with N27s wage cut, only the shitty side of town was available.

At the bus stop, Ethan found a medical pamphlet about heart conditions. The comparison chart didn't have a gauge for over-weight skaters with anxiety issues. He couldn't even feel his pulse in his wrist for a while, but when he did, he timed the beats and counted 78. The leaflet said, people with 78 bpm needed to watch out for something until he spilt his can of Coke over it and couldn't read the lettering. It didn't matter. He didn't need a leaflet to tell him he was under pressure.

Getting into the leisure centre was much easier this time when he hadn't lost his board over the fence. Reed had told him of another way to get in further around the perimeter, but Ethan couldn't be bothered with the walk. As he cut across the field towards the caravan, he saw Reed sitting outside on the camping chair.

'You're late,' he said.

Ethan checked, 'Only by ten minutes. What did I miss?'

'Let me tell you how this is going to go.' Reed slapped his thighs and stood. 'I'll tell you what to do and you do it. No complaints. No back-chat.'

'Yes, boss,' Ethan saluted. 'However, I was hoping to work together. You help me, I help you, etcetera.'

'How?' Reed unzipped the bag of pads and threw over a set of yellow ones. 'I'm your short-cut to success according to you.'

It was the only time he wished for a pair with a little more dirt on them. 'Do you have anything in black?' Ethan sized the pads up against his trousers and reluctantly strapped them on. 'The sooner I get this beast under control, the sooner I can shoot my edit and get out of here.'

'I don't see any camera.'

'My filmer can't make it.' Dixel left another message on Ethan's phone to say she wouldn't be able to join him but would be there tomorrow. It was an empty promise as far as he was concerned. One thing he hated more than lies were empty promises. He wanted to show her the complex, the abandoned architecture, see the pool, and meet Reed. 'Believe me when I say that pools aren't on the top of my list to ride. I'd rather be anywhere other than here.'

'The feeling is mutual,' Reed said. 'I want you to be anywhere other than here, too. Whatever happened to wanting to learn an Invert?'

Ethan blew through his teeth as if he couldn't even imagine it.

'And don't forget to tighten the straps,' Reed said.

'Nah. I can't bend my legs properly as it is. How am I supposed to learn anything if I can't move?'

'Your first mistake.'

'Three strikes and I'm out?' Ethan jumped down into the pool. 'I'll take the risk. Let's do this.' He expected some kind of instruction, but looked back and saw Reed doing lunges.

'You need to stretch first.' He jumped up and down on the spot and swung his arms around in circles.

'No. *You* need to warm up. I'm good to go.'

'Your second mistake.'

'I'm really racking up the points.'

Whilst Reed stretched out on the side, Ethan got the feel of the pool, carving around, scratching the coping occasionally, and popping some small ollies half-way up in the deep end.

'Right. I'm warmed up. Let's start with that Invert?'

'No. Start with the basics: Pumping.'

Ethan rode the pool like it was a mini ramp and Reed knew it. If he didn't learn to pump correctly, he wouldn't be able to gain any speed and impress anyone. The secret was in the pumping. Get that; get everything else.

Reed grabbed Ethan's board as he walked past him and pulled out a spanner.

'Don't…' Reed turned the spanner a full 360 on his kingpin, '… loosen them,' Ethan said.

It felt like a wobble-board afterwards. 'Keep an eye on that spanner.' Ethan got back in the pool. 'I'm going to need it again in a minute.'

'First,' Reed said. 'I'll show you how to do it. Watch my head. Look past the transitions not at them.' He pushed off into a simple carve around the deep end. Smoother and faster than Ethan's attempts. It was as if he was on a track, gliding down, up, around, and back again, without any adjustment for the coping. 'Look beyond the lip.'

Whatever the hell that meant.

Reed continued calling out instructions as he flew around the pool, including: follow the line, look up, use your head, lean back, lean forward, and anticipate the corner don't wait for it. After two loops around the bowl, the itch to ride was in his feet. *Got it*, Ethan thought, *My turn*, but again Reed followed the same line, over and over, pump after pump.

'OK, I've got it!' Ethan shouted.

Reed shot around the shallow end then passed for another carve. 'And take note of my arms.'

Ethan couldn't see his arms doing anything worth remembering. 'I'm bored now,' he said, just as Reed came to a stop. 'About time.' He couldn't wait to hear any more instructions and rolled off into the deep end. He tried to match the same line and speed but ended up doing what he always did and pivoted off his back truck. More instructions arrived, all thick and lumpy: *You've got trucks: use them*; *Don't lean back; More arms; Use your toes*; and the classic, *Look ahead*. If this was training, he wanted a full refund. He tried again but just felt like an idiot.

'Get on your toes earlier and stop kick-turning.'

Instructions arrived and created more Resistance, until eventually, it crumbled into Submission. Anything to shut the man up. It was nice not to think about slamming on some fiddly trick. Ethan's calves burned, but as he pushed through the loops, a thought snuck into his head about the final edit.

He's in a pool—a real one. Even a crappy edit is going to be watched like crazy. His old crew would see it and be surprised. *He's changed*, they'd say. *He's not the same. Let's call him up again.*

'You're still doing it wrong.' Reed got into the pool as Ethan came to a stop. Apparently, there was a big invisible line on the floor which Reed pointed at, and he needed to follow. 'You're looking at the floor,' he said. 'Look at where you want to go.'

As soon as Ethan tried to follow that invisible line, the damn thing disappeared. He got a little higher on the hip, kept his speed under control, but missed the line time and time again.

'Focus on your arms,' Reed said. 'Swing them ahead of you…' He ran up the transition. 'Head, arms, chest, then legs. Tighten up at the apex, feel the transition, let the pump carry you through it.'

The advice worked, eventually, as Ethan hit the magic combination, suddenly he felt a whoosh of speed.

'That was it,' Reed shouted. 'Do it again.'

'I don't know what I did!' Again, Ethan hit the hip and the deep end, but it just came around at his usual slow speed. After another try, he caught it again. 'Got it.' Another attempt. 'Missed it.'

'Keep going.' Reed went back to his chair and poured out a drink from a flask. Ethan came to a halt in the shallow end. 'Why are you stopping?' Reed asked.

'I'm done.' Ethan kicked his board away and sat in the shade of the transition.

'That's another thing we need to talk about: your stamina.'

Give it a rest.

10

—

A STRANGE ARRIVAL

The Martins hopped across the bushes in the distance and Ethan hoped to see the blurry figure of Dixel making her way over. The disappointment slowed his breath and he wondered if all the effort was worth it. After all, no camera, no point. Knowing Reed's history didn't help. For a man who didn't want to acknowledge him, he now sure had a lot to say. He'd grown up in Bristol, moved away with the Army, came back and everything had changed: the centre had been rebuilt, the gentrification had moved in, friends had moved away, and the rest hadn't changed a bit. He realised it was him who had changed, not the city. His relationship failed, he couldn't hold down his packing job in the factory, and he eventually found himself on the streets. It wasn't even difficult, as he'd roughed it much worse. He even preferred it. One man's homelessness is another man's minimalism.

A Land Rover had pulled up in a lay-by across the field. Reed noticed it first. A short dark-haired overweight man in a white shirt and too much jewellery strolled in their direction.

'Someone you know?' Ethan asked.

The man put a friendly hand up and Reed began walking over. They spoke for a minute or two, looked towards the caravan, and pointed at the leisure centre a couple of times. There was a polite distance between the men, but not enough to invite him over to the pool. The man laughed at the end of everything he said, eventually shook hands, and returned to his vehicle.

'Who was that?'

'Their car broke down yesterday.' Reed sat down again. 'I helped them with it. He said he just looking around. I have a bad feeling about that guy.'

'Don't I know it.' Ethan sniffed out a thought. 'Someone is making my life difficult. Every time I have to film one of these edits, something big goes wrong. Just once I'd like to have a smooth sail, but it never happens. It's fishy.'

'Any ideas who it might be?'

'Nope.'

'What's the link?'

'I don't have one yet. It's a different place and a different problem each time.'

Reed thought for a moment, then said, 'Who decides where you go?'

'My brother.'

'Do you get on with him?'

Ethan was taken aback by the idea, 'Yeah, of course.'

'OK, sorry. I was only asking.'

After a moment of quiet passed, the attention turned back to the pool and Reed's lesson continued. Ethan halted the noise by rolling away again. The session which followed seemed to go much better. Though Reed told him to stop trying so hard and to stop thinking about the curves. Pools were about feeling the board and letting it go wherever it wanted. If he went too fast, he could either tighten up and stay low and fast, or let the arc push him higher into a grind. Ethan rarely wanted to stay low, but that coping was a challenge. Reed might have seen one smooth edge, but Ethan just saw gravestone keys on a piano played by Death. Those gaps may have been close, but it was disconcerting to feel the click under his board, unlike like the smooth metal coping he was used to. With practice, he made progress, but that didn't mean he was enjoying it.

Reed told him to not do any tricks yet, and to keep the grinds simple. Flat walls were a gift compared to the curves of a pool; Ethan never had to think about the lip of a ramp, ever. He tested a frontside fifty-fifty over the steps, and after surviving that, he took the same trick backside into the deep.

'I'm getting the hang of it.' As if tempting fate wasn't enough, Ethan whizzed past Reed on the hip. 'I'll go for something else.'

He launched a frontside ollie clean out of the top, a simple arc, popped, caught, and guided in an effortless, bearing-hum rotation, until he saw his landing. He hadn't allowed for the curved coping. He was on a course to clip his wheels and despite trying to compress and suck it up, it wasn't enough. The front truck cleared, but not the back. The coping ripped the board out from under him, his legs followed, and he slammed into the transition at the bottom.

It felt like all his organs tumbled around like numbers in a lottery draw, and once they'd settled, they weren't in the winning order. Ethan rolled around on the flat, groaning.

'I told you not to try any tricks,' Reed said. 'And mistake number three: you should have stretched.'

He wanted to get back on it, but that pain wouldn't shift, and as soon as he saw the lump on his hip, he knew the session was over.

Reed gave him a couple of frozen pigeons

wrapped in a towel to ice it. 'I've got to defrost them anyway. Let's try again tomorrow.'

'If this isn't killing me.'

'I've got some hip padding you can borrow.'

This is turning into Gladiators.

Despite the pain and hideous pad choice, Reed's invitation to return was welcome. The practice was starting to pay off.

'I'll be later tomorrow,' Ethan said, 'as it's Sunday bus times.'

'How about you skate here?' Reed nodded at Ethan's stomach. 'You need it.'

The point hurt, though he didn't show it. He knew he wasn't as fit as he was, but there was no need to chip away at a man's self-esteem. So much for black being a slimming colour. Still, he was ready. Quips like this had been aimed at his belly for the past year and he'd built up a list of one-liners in defence: it's all muscle, the perspective of my shadow, the way I'm standing, I might be fat, but at least I'm not fifty.

Before they parted company Reed spit-balled one more idea. 'I've been thinking about what you said: you think you're being set up. Do you realise the only consistent thing each time, is you?'

'You think I'm causing this myself?'

'No. But the only thing you can control in this

world is yourself. I heard someone smart say once, the definition of insanity is doing the same thing over and over again and expecting a different result.'

'I don't know what you mean.'

'Whatever you normally do, next time, don't. Do something different.'

Life would be easier if people said what they meant. Instead, the words pin-balled around trying to form sentences he could read between. He thought about Reed, his motives, and why he said what he said. Then he thought about the change he needed to make until he realised he was doing hard math again.

'Ok, I'll think about it.'

'Or,' Reed added, 'maybe you are going insane.' He took out a couple of pills from his medicine bottle and sank them with a gulp of water.

11

A BLACKER MOMENT

The next day at N27, Ethan was late, and there was a feeling of anticipation in the air.

'The new boss is here,' old Eric said. 'He's very nice. Not a bit like I'd thought he'd be. Everyone seems to like him.'

'Great.' Ethan scribbled the name *Mickey Mouse* into the signing in book. Signing in and out of the building was now a thing. Health and Safety they called it. The only benefit was that it's easy to discover who was in the building. He flicked back over a page and found Dixel's name.

'Where is he now?'

'Looping the building on a tour. He'll be back here shortly.'

Blacker's arrival could be a good moment to impress. There was only ever a small window of opportunity to truly speak your mind in a company and that was on day one. After that, peoples' routines would bed down like sediment over the choppy surface of their personalities, passing him from meeting to meeting, feeding him so many glossy perspectives that the company finish would appear brand new. If this guy was as good as Eric thinks, then he could become an ally, unlike Flint. It'll be nice to have someone on his side for once.

The clicking of heels on a polished floor echoed towards him out of a corridor. It sounded like a time-bomb arriving and meant it was too late to escape.

'This'll be him now.' Eric moved to the back of reception to allow the more important employees ample opportunity to gather round. As the crowds formed, Eric almost got pushed out of the building. The whole of the fourth floor circled a female speaker: Annette from HR. Behind her was a slim man in his early fifties with bushy, but well-kept black and grey hair. The lines in his forehead yanked up his eyebrows like a Venetian blind; an adorable cheek-mole screamed, *make-up department*. After Annette had said her piece, the room clapped right on schedule, and some idiot even took photos of a handshake for the company newsletter. Eventually, the room calmed their delirium right on cue so the man could speak.

· · ·

'Blah. Blah-blah-blah.'
Smile.
Applause.
'Blah blah, blah. Blah. Blah. Blah-blah blah.'
Smile.
Applause.

Ethan sat on a chrome bin by the pillar, took off his shoe, and used the lace end to pick out the dried mud from his tread. It was like a riverbed of pale brown happiness in there, with bits popping out and landing on the carpet with each dig and flick. Many of the pieces landed on his hoodie and looked like miniature versions of the pellet feed you can buy for £1 a bag at the city farm. There were about two hundred snaking crevices per shoe at a guess, not all of them muddied up, but plenty to be fiddling with whilst the ass-kissing continued.

The talk consisted of meaningless statements, rhetorical questions, pauses for reflection, exaggerated hand gestures, valley-girl style tonal inflexions, and an eyewink to a certain someone in the front row who got the in-joke. Someone giggled. Everyone laughed.

Round of applause.

The daylight faded and a horseshoe of perspiration rainbows gathered until Ethan realised Annette and Blacker were standing in front of him

'This is Ethan Wares.' Annette smiled hard at Ethan, who reluctantly slid off the bin and flicked shoe dirt on the floor. 'He's one of the Youth Entertainment team who's been with us for about a year now; he's been producing excellent content for the brand.'

A smile appeared as if someone had clamped a bulldog clip on the back of Blacker's head, and a spring-loaded handshake bounced into position. Ethan wiped his clean hand on his filthy trousers and slapped it into the MDs hand before someone could say sanitiser. Blacker's grip was firm, as if the last email he'd typed was a complaint. Ethan squeezed until he heard some knuckles crack, then he pulled it towards him like a political psychopath and threw it back like a bad hand at poker.

The conversation died and a breathy wheeze of laughter huffed out between Blacker's cheeks. 'Great to meet you,' he said. 'I'll be paying a visit to all departments soon to find out more about what everyone does here.' His knuckle crunched hand scurried away into a trouser pocket.

With the meet and greet closed, everyone was invited out for an early lunch. Blacker insisted they go on without him whilst he made a quick call. Whoops of joy ricocheted off everyone's foreheads and one by one a Conga line of smiles and chatter snaked out of reception. The likelihood of *lunch* consisting of a sandwich was low. They'd probably end up in the Lebanese Restaurant across the road, picking various mouth-burning dishes from a menu no-one can read.

Instead, Ethan headed for the Editing & Mixing suites to find Dixel. These small rooms were usually locked if audios needed to be recorded, but that early lunch offer created a row of green lights above each door. Wendy, from Marketing, faffed with a heavy box on some sack trucks outside the IT store. She offset the threat of sweat on her brow by hitting the Fire Exit handle and asked Ethan for light. He padded his pockets and realised he'd left his zippo in the leisure centre somewhere.

'Sorry, I've got nothing,' he said. 'I've quit by the way.'

'Since when?'

'For a couple of months now.'

'Don't give me all that *health* nonsense.' Wendy dug about in some drawers until she found lighter. 'I mean, I know it's killing me, but I like it. I feel great. I literally can't start the day without one.'

'What's in the box?' Ethan opened the lid. 'iPads?'

'We've all been upgraded, so these are no longer needed.' She pressed the lighter against her bottom lip. 'I don't suppose you'd want to help me reset them, would you?'

He took one out and opened its cover. They were immaculate.

'I mean. You'd be doing me a massive favour.'

'How many are there?' There appeared to be at least two dozen. 'Let me keep one as payment.'

'You're a star,' Wendy beamed. 'Go for it. These things go *missing* all the time, anyways.' She hugged Ethan and headed for the door.

'Where are you going?'

'Lunch. The new guy is paying,' she said, then, 'You get started and I'll join you later. Thanks, Hun.'

And just like that, a quick job suddenly became a much slower one. Wendy would probably forget to return and eventually arrive when he'd finished the lot. He slid the box across the floor to the desk, lifted the iPads out, and began powering them on.

The rooms to all the editing suites were locked but for the last door: security, and naturally it was unlocked. Whoever was on shift must have been out on their rounds. No sign of Dixel either. She might have finished for the morning, but it was barely ten forty-five. It would be good if she responded to his texts. Two sent yesterday and three this morning. All of them read, but none replied to.

The monotony of resetting the iPads soon set in: log in with the guest pin-code, go to *Settings*, turn off, *Find My Device*, start the Reset, confirm the reset, and wait. One done; twenty-three to go. The good thing about monotony is the opportunity to switch off and think about something else. That something else was Reed and that pool. Technically, having a mentor to learn how to ride it was unnecessary. Sure, it was nice, but in no way essential. At least there was someone to ride with. It was unbelievable that the caravan had been his home for a decade. The council woman said that he fixed and sold mechanical parts, but if he was in the army, or even ex-army, it seemed crazy to live like that.

The tedium of completing just four iPads was enough. The others just looked like a waste of time and besides were not his responsibility. Technically, Wendy had pulled a fast one on him, however, her plan slipped up by believing Ethan cared about wiping any of them, let alone all of them.

One of the office doors in the hallway clicked shut. The security guard was back. It was Dennis.

Ethan opened the door and leant on the frame.

'You're still here then.' Dennis leant back in his chair and his elbow hit a switch. The voice of Blacker came through the speakers.

It's a complete shamble here. The whole place needs shutting down.

. . .

Blacker was on one of the screens being broadcasted from an interview room. His grainy self, phone to his ear, hand on hip, pacing around a room. Dennis quickly tried to silence the call but wasn't sure which switch he knocked.

Most of middle management needs to go; I've got a team I can bring in… Give me twenty-four hours…

Dennis killed the feed, 'Sorry about that. What were you saying?' He ripped open his packet sandwiches.

'Uh.' Ethan looked away from the frozen image of Blacker on the screen. 'I've been looking for you. Where have you come from?' That clip was golden. He had to have it.

'From the reservoir. Why?'

'I've just come from the Westside and there's a bunch of guys hanging out near the gates. They look dodgy as hell.'

Dennis went to the monitors and called up the CCTV camera. 'They seem to have gone now.'

'Seriously,' Ethan said. 'I wouldn't leave it as Blacker's about.'

'You're right.' Dennis put down his sandwiches and made for the door. 'Radio me if you see anyone on any of the other screens.'

'Will do.' Ethan watched him run down the corridor until he heard the click and slam of the door unlocking and locking again. He sat in Dennis' chair, found the monitor controller for screen 8, and found the recording of Blacker. He played a little of it forward and then found the endpoint: 3 minutes 43 seconds. He highlighted the sequence, hit the export to mp4 button, and dropped the file on to a blank 4 gig USB stick he found in the in-tray. Once it had finished copying across, he ejected the stick and left the room. He didn't know what he was going to do with it if anything at all, but something like that was too good to ignore.

He thought about what Blacker had said. Middle management covered a broad line of people. It seemed as if everyone in N27 was middle management to some degree. He wasn't, neither was Dixel, but Heston? Maybe he was. Project Manager sure sounded like it. Ethan decided to reset one more iPad, though really, he just waited for Dennis to return. He put one iPad in his bag then packed the handful he'd completed back in the box with a note on top to say he had to shoot. On the walkout through reception, he met Daniella and Clare from Accounts on their way back from the restaurant. They smelt Lebanese.

'Can you tell me who's eating with Blacker?'

'Duh,' said Daniella. 'Everyone, but you, it seems.'

'Was Dixel there?'

'Didn't see her.' They headed to the lift, then Clare said, 'If you want to join them, they're sitting in the fireplace.'

'No. I'm good.' Ethan felt for the USB stick in his pocket and headed off.

12

GYPSIES

The arrival back at the pool that afternoon had an ominous start: the double gates to the leisure centre had been yanked from their fittings and lay flattened and buckled by fresh tyre tracks. That shiny new padlock was untouched and still attached, as if messing with it was too much hassle. On rounding the corner of the main building Ethan saw a dozen or so vehicles had set themselves up in a group in the field. Kids played games around the bushes whilst some adults shifted boxes from one vehicle to another.

He made his way quickly across the field hopping from bush to bush to keep his presence to a minimum. When he reached the pool, he jumped down out of sight. Reed must have been out as the caravan's windows were slightly open for the dogs and the curtains were shut all around. They'd planned to meet at 10 am, and as Ethan was on time, something must have pulled Reed away.

Dixel was also supposed to be there but wasn't.

Once in the pool, there was nothing to do but wait. And waiting meant riding. The second day of riding felt a bit more familiar, even if it was annoying to ride solo. It still felt more like work than fun. His heart wasn't really in it and the effort to try a trick when the frickin' thing could spit him to the flat whenever it wanted, felt pointless. Better to wait for someone to arrive.

During a pause in his roll, he figured he'd try Dixel again. When she answered it was obvious she hadn't even made it out of bed.

'You're late,' he said.

'Sorry,' she yawned. 'I had to work late last night and didn't get home until two.'

'But you're still coming, right? I mean, you can get here for 10.30?'

'I can't. I've got to go back in. I'm backed up and the deadline isn't moving.'

'We've only got a couple of days to get this done.'

'I know, but give me a break. We can do it tomorrow.'

'You said you'd be here.'

'Yeah, and now I can't.'

'You promised.'

'Are you ten or something? I didn't promise

anything. I said I'd be there and now I can't. I'll get there when I can, but it isn't going to be today.'

Ethan went quiet. He was seething inside and on the verge of losing his shit. If Dixel could see him, she'd see a man pacing around the flat of the pool, silently swearing at his phone, composing himself then speaking calmly again.

'There's no chance you can make it today, at all?'

'Flint didn't like the edit I produced. I was working there so late I fell asleep at the desk. I've got to get in there again this morning. Wait, what time is it?'

'Just gone ten-fifteen.'

'Damn it. I'm late. Look, I'll speak to you later, I've got to go.'

'Wait!'

Dixel hung up.

Bang went his plan for the day with the swift click of a call cutting out.

Go Figure.

It bothered Ethan that he had no leverage with Dixel. At least with his mates, he could wind them up, call them out, talk shit, and let them deal with it. Always friendly, though, even if they couldn't take it. He, Chris, and Elliott were on equal footing on the food chain, so their conversations would mouse around the maze all day and *never* find the exit. The world Dixel came from was a whole lot different than his, and her words were sharp, and her thoughts were fast. He hated having his speech stoppered with truths, but she was good at it.

Still, the edit was due soon and Blacker was looking for a reason to slay anyone with a weakness: management or not. If the edit wasn't submitted in the next day or two, then the deadline squeeze would be on. The threat: Ricard Flint. Another week and another submission of his *Line Life* cut could pick up enough views to poke its head onto the radar of Change.

With Helplessness, ideas arrived quick and stupid mashed together like warm playdough, to form a *new* shape called, Desperation. He had a phone: why not film his own part? The Network wouldn't normally accept phone footage, but if Ricard could submit it, why couldn't he?

Drop-in some filters, picture in picture framing, a collage or something, and it would work. Kids these days were sharing any old, filtered crap and getting hits. Surely, it was worth a shot? Maybe Reed was good enough with a camera? Or maybe he had a camera? He was full of surprises so far, despite being a few currants short of a pancake. Maybe he'd fixed a frickin' video camera in that collection of his. Anything could be hidden away in there.

Just when Ethan decided to jump back on his

board again, a kid around twelve-years-old walked up to the edge of the pool.

'Don't stand too close,' Ethan said. 'You don't want to fall in.'

The kid put a cigarette to his lips, dragged on it like he had a forty-fags-a-day habit, and blew out a cartoon speech bubble. 'What the hell are you doing in that hole?' His Irish accent was so strong Ethan needed subtitles to pick out the consonants.

He pointed to his setup. 'Skateboarding.'

'What do you want to do that for?'

'Fun.'

'Fun? You're a grown man. Shouldn't you be at work or something?' The kid turned and called over a dozen rats of various ages until the side of the pool was a silhouette of buzz cuts squinting at this strange new species they'd found. A few girls gathered too. One was about eighteen with long dark hair and a dusting of cute freckles.

'Show us something then,' she said.

'Don't talk to him, Nan,' the first kid said. 'He's up to no good there. Look at him; the dirty feck.'

'Shut up, Darragh,' Nan said. 'Go on. Show us.'

Some of the other kids also wanted to see him ride. Darragh tried to silence them like a ringleader, but they were having none of it.

There was no getting away from the two useless choices, so Ethan picked the better one and rolled into the deep end. He carved his familiar figure of eight and made sure to time the pump at the right point for speed. He even managed to forget the kids and enjoy himself. His legs felt good, the timing was getting there, and the pump whipped him around high and fast. The kids loved it when he got up on the coping thinking that he was about to fall off. The cheers switched from *Yays* to *Ooos* pre-empting some danger. It was tempting to give them a proper show with something more technical, but the speed alone appeared to satisfy their interest. As he finished up his run a voice shouted down at him.

'Is that it?' Darragh said. 'I've seen better.'

'I thought it was good,' Nan said. She'd walked around to the steps 'Give us a go, will you?' She stepped onto Ethan's board and grabbed his shoulder to steady herself. Her arms were soft, and her hair smelt of coconut shampoo.

'Don't you touch her.' Darragh jumped into the pool. 'Or I'll batter you.'

'Leave it, Darragh.' Nan rolled a little, wobbled a lot, lost her balance, and pulled on Ethan's arms as she stepped off. Her friends wolf-whistled and laughed which only wound Darragh up more.

'Cut it out.' He pulled Nan away and pushed Ethan back. 'I told you to stay off her. If you're needing a beating, I'm gunna give you one.' The boy threw his cigarette at him and took up a boxing stance with his fists. 'C'mon on now. I'll batter you senseless.'

More kids joined their friends at the top of the pool, as if they'd arrived via a conveyor belt, and immediately encouraged the fight. Ethan held his palms up, stepped back, and tried to calm the tension, even though he wanted to slap the kid. Darragh edged forward and threw some jabs into the fresh air, weaving like a boxer.

'I'm not fighting you,' Ethan said.

Darragh dropped his hands, 'Too right you're not fighting me. You're a sissy-boy, ain't you?'

Ethan side-stepped Darragh's attempt to spit at him. He wanted to rewind time and be alone again in the pool. If there was ever a time for Reed to arrive and provide backup, now would be good. Some of the kids realised that nothing was going to happen and calmed their thirst for a fight. The numbers fell away from the pool edge and attention moved towards the caravan. Darragh was the last to leave and only climbed out once he felt he had control of the situation. When there was no-one left to show-off to, it was over.

'If I see you around here chasing after Nancy, I'm going to kill you. You hear me? This is ours now.' He pointed to the whole field, then backed away from the lip. Nancy joined her friends, who all found the whole event hilarious as they walked off towards the camp. The boys soon followed the girls back, bickering amongst themselves.

Ethan tried to ride a little more, but after ten

minutes he realised that Reed might be hours, and Dixel wasn't showing. Not only that, but he didn't want to risk another spat with the gypsy kids. He still had Kirsty's card on him, and the thought occurred that maybe she could help. That camp wasn't going to move on quickly and he didn't want to go through all this again tomorrow.

13

THE VKNG

The council offices hummed with enough desk fans to keep sweat particles circulating and the paper-work sticky. A lump of Blu Tack on the desk of Kirsty Sapsford sparkled with the disco-ball gloss of Muffin crumbs. And you just know they were fresh on this morning.

Heather from reception removed the tissue paper from inside a brand-new white mug. 'Would you like a cup of tea?' She blew the dust away with a layer of spit breath and flashed a wide smile. Neurones needed to align to reply, but before Ethan could, she added, 'Kirsty will be back shortly. She's just in a meeting.' Then, 'How many sugars?' And shook the mug handle like it contained charitable donations measured in teabags for her annual review. He didn't have the heart to deny her all that excitement in the kitchen.

Once she'd glided away in a dress long enough to hide her shoes, Ethan glanced around Kirsty's workstation. Everything had a *Shape* name and logo on following the council rebrand. The Marketing Department must have hosed money around like a flamethrower to stamp that brand into the staff psyche: pads of paper, pencils and pens, ruler, eraser, calculator, monitor sticker, mouse mat. Ethan slid open a drawer and saw the same logo on a snap-back cap, a bottle opener, and what appeared to be a Frisbee.

When Kirsty eventually got back to her desk, she found him soaking up spilt tea with a Shape hand towel from her bottom drawer.

'Oh, don't worry about it,' she said. 'We've got lots more in the store cupboard. What can I do for you?'

He explained about the Gypsy camp at the leisure centre and was met with hoisted eyebrows and pinched lips. The need to get them off-site had a priority which required a red phone and a direct line to an action team. The trouble was Kirsty's desk didn't appear to have the necessary equipment. As the gravitas of the situation dawned, her eyebrows slowly lowered back into position.

'The procedure for getting a group removed from a site is not easy,' she stressed. 'Paperwork will need to be completed and submitted in triplicate.' Forms were gathered quickly from the *Shit Which*

Happens All The Time drawer and handed over with all the joy of Snowdrops in Spring.

The thickness of paper between his fingers didn't need counting. 'All of it?' he asked.

'The sooner you submit the application, the better, but you'll need to be patient.' She offered him some Bourbon biscuits from a Tupperware container. The partially lifted lid corner closed low and quick as if exposing them further would break some office code. 'Travellers have been known to occupy land for years without a sufficient challenge. If your case is strong enough, you'll be looking at months, at best.'

'There's no other way?' he asked.

Her leg crossed at the knee, a shoe balanced from her toes, and a varicose vein teased his gag-reflex. 'Sadly not. They have rights just like everyone else. It's unfortunate they're on a site that you and your friends also want to use, but you shouldn't really be there either. There's not much I can do,' she paused. 'Unless.'

'Unless?'

'They could choose to move on by themselves.'

That was the glimmer of hope he needed. 'Ok, great. How?'

'I don't know. Maybe they're just passing through?' She double-clicked on her mouse and logged into her computer. 'I'm afraid I've got to get back to work, but if you see Joel can you ask him to contact me. I know you think he can handle the winter in that caravan, but I'm not so sure.'

'You know he's served in the Army, right?'

'Is that what he's told you?' It was one of those questions which didn't need an answer. 'Please ask him to contact me. That flat is too good to lose.'

Those forms cut him in two. The last time he handled paperwork of any importance, it was his homework to give it to his old mate Bryon Dunkley. They had a mutually beneficial friendship built around secondary school Economics of demand and supply. Ethan sorted out the morons demanding Bryon's lunch money and Bryon supplied Ethan's completed homework in return.

Four years later, Ethan knew he had to track down Bryon again.

German techno beats hammered from the open windows of The Vkng Pub. Its vowel teeth were knocked out to repel a generation north of fifty, who played skittles there for decades, hugged pints of weak, flat bitter all night, and fought to hold on to their chairs until defeat of youth overwhelmed them. Now the once quiet end of Hadyn Street crackled with ladies' heels on cobbles, who squealed and wobbled their way through the evening, tipsy on Prosecco and vodka shots.

The *Club*room opened at 10 pm and the queue

to get in was already longer than expected. There was a bonus of short skirts and summer dresses available, but Ethan couldn't linger, as the bouncers knew his face wouldn't fit in with their clientele. He pulled aside a hipster at the back and bribed him twenty pounds to open the window near the rear fire exit. The guy took the money quickly and probably figured he wouldn't see the stranger anymore that night.

'Thanks, pal. See you inside.' then, 'Great look by the way: very memorable and so easy to pick out in a crowd.' Ethan slapped him hard on the shoulder then x-rayed his face whilst all the pennies dropped.

A couple argued at the front of the queue, distracting the doormen, allowing Ethan to peel away from the crowd and watch from across the road. Bryon always loved techno and it was an easy guess that The Vkng's beats would call him like a siren. Ethan scrolled through his contacts and called his old friend's number. The call connected but went to voicemail. It was a good sign: the number was still active.

It took fifteen long minutes for Ethan's man to get into the pub and start his walk around the back of the building. A couple were snogging up against the emergency exit which would have been cute and comfortable to see at a hundred metres on a sunny day in a park, but up close, not so much. He pulled their suction apart with a little persuasion and pushed them towards the streetlights away from the dark confusion of the alley.

The fire exit wait stretched out thin and frayed at the edges with tension by the time the window popped open. As soon as the guy leant out for a look, Ethan caught hold of the window frame, grabbed the man's jacket, and used it to haul himself through.

'You took your time.' Ethan stepped down off the fire extinguisher.

'No, I was coming, I just got caught up, that was all.' The air between them should have faded away, but it fermented into a thick silence. 'You mentioned an extra twenty?' The man asked.

'I've been out there for twenty minutes.' Which wasn't technically a lie. The guy's mouth swung open with all the *duhs* queuing up in his head as Ethan shook his hand, said *Thanks*, and made his way out into the Pub.

The bar was busy with people holding tenners for a drink, and Ethan found a spot at one end to keep an eye out for Bryon's face. After a few minutes of watching money exchange hands, a heavily wrist-banded hand collected a pair of drinks from the barman. A tattoo of an A on the wrist triggered a memory, but he couldn't put a face or name to the owner. The crowd danced and jostled around blocking his view of the group of men. A packet of Rizzla's dropped on the floor and a male stood to re-join the banter; they spotted each other. The sunken-eyed lad was the local pill dealer Charlie Deakin.

A singular Deakin out of his comfort zone was a dull, pathetic, shit-bag with a nasal voice that sounded like a Disney character. Spending any longer than five minutes in the guy's company would irritate the hell out of anyone. However, one alcohol powered Deakin in the company of his friends led him to believe he was some kind of 6ix9ine gangster. Ethan ducked out of sight, but it was too late. The kaleidoscope memory of his weed debt lit up like a runway between them and guided Deakin and his crew towards their cash bonus.

Ethan scuttled low across the dance floor, bashed into the legs of some people, and bumped into a table of drinkers on his way to the hallway. He vaulted down the stairs into the chill-out space, sprinted through to the back, and turned into the Gents. Out of breath, he lurched up against the sinks and waited for someone to barge in through the door. After a minute of silence, apart from someone having a difficult birth in the stall, he relaxed a little. Reed was right about his stamina; he was getting out of shape faster than ever. He splashed cold water on his face, then felt someone grab his collar and yank him violently backwards.

'You owe me,' Deakin shouted into his face. His

eyes struggled to settle like he'd been testing the merchandise a little too much.

Ethan rubbed his wet face. 'Leave it out.' There were four goons behind Deakin, which meant the battle-math of survival equalled a good beating at least.

'You better have a lot of money on you.' A punch followed, straight into Ethan's stomach, which took him by surprise and sent the pair to the floor wrestling in a stench of urine and lemon blocks. The goons let them get on with it but kept intervening whenever Ethan got the upper hand. Deakin's punches were nothing more than pathetic jabs and glance blows; he was such a crap fighter. As he stood, Ethan swept his legs and sent him back to the floor. The goons picked Ethan up and threw him at the cubical door. It broke off its hinges to the surprise of a guy snorting something off the back of the water tank. Ethan saw the birthmark on his cheek.

'Bryon?'

'Wares?' Bryon flicked white power from his nose. He'd doubled in size from when Ethan had last seen him and must have married a tanning bed too.

Deakin continued his kicks as Ethan did his best to deflect them away from his body.

'A little help here?' Ethan asked.

Two powerful hands pushed hard in the middle

of Deakin's chest and thrust him out through the cubical into the sinks. Bryon, in a tight Hawaiian shirt and highlights, stepped out and pushed Deakin again, whiplashing his head against the mirrors. Deakin fell, concussed to the floor. Two of Deakin's friends ran back out through the toilet doors, and the other two held up their hands in immediate surrender and slowly backed away. Bryon didn't even bother to threaten them further and went back to help Ethan up.

'Are you ok?'

Ethan felt his neck crunch a little when he rotated it. The dizzy specks in his vision slowly disappeared. 'I barely recognised you. You look like you've been eating the gym.'

'A lot of time has passed.' Bryon studied his hair in the mirror and pushed a few loose ends back into position.

Deakin began to groan back to life.

'Shall we go?' Ethan asked.

'If we have to,' Bryon said. 'Though you have just made the night more interesting.'

14

BRYON'S HELP

The Crown was just a few doors down from The Vkng. The pair found a seat in the window with a wobbly table whilst a covers band played at the back of the room. They made small talk about life since they last met, but Ethan skipped a lot of details. The past was not a happy place to recall, so he glossed over most of his details to remain a vague blur.

Bryon moved the menus to the side of the table and asked about the car accident. 'What are the chances of someone having a heart attack whilst driving?' He stirred a pint of iced water with a slice of lime. 'And that kid? I guess the health and safety regs on child seats have got better over the years.'

Ethan wanted to get off the topic as sooner or later it would turn to the subject of Heston's compensation package. It always did.

'I need a favour,' Ethan interrupted. 'I've got to apply to the council to get some gypsies removed from the old leisure centre and…'

Bryon pushed back into his seat and smiled. 'Nothing changes, does it? You still want me to do your homework.'

'It's not like I've got any smarter since school.' A thought itched Bryon and Ethan saw it. 'What?'

'You know how many people have kept in contact after leaving?'

He couldn't even guess.

'None,' Bryon said. 'I mean, school sucks, I get that, but I don't want it erased from my life.' Ethan removed the papers from his jacket, unfolded them out on the table, which Bryon reluctantly took and leafed through. When he'd finished looking at them, he placed them back on the table. 'We need to leave,' he said.

'Already?' Ethan stood and tried to sink a full pint as fast as he could.

They took the canal path through the town whilst Bryon explained he'd been surfing a lot on the North Devon coast and moved away to be nearer the M5. 'I've also been temping whilst I try to figure out what I want to do.'

'You kept up with the electronics?' Ethan asked.

'No. It was my dad's business, not mine.'

'Where are we going by the way?'

'Another sixty seconds and you'll see.'

The pair turned into the gateway of a compound with El Gato's truck inside.

'You work for El Gato?'

'Who?'

'Edwardo Hermanez.'

'You know him?'

Bryon walked past the office door and around the side of the building.

'You're not going inside?'

'I am, but it's alarmed, and I don't have my key.' Bryon removed a small panel from the wall and used a thin tool in the lock to wriggle and pop the door off. Inside was the alarm system. He took the front plate off with a small screwdriver, and pulled two pairs of cables, bent them into a pinch, and bit off the plastic coating. He then went to a car in the compound, took out a spare key from under the wheel arch, unlocked the boot, removed a pair of jump leads, opened the bonnet, and disconnected a spark plug lead. One end of the jump leads connected to the battery and the other attached to the bare wires of the alarm system. 'You get in the car and when I say go: start the engine,' Bryon said.

Ethan looked at the old Ford and felt the sweat on his palms.

'I'm bypassing the alarm sensor. I need you to turn the engine over, to cause a power to dip for a few seconds, then I can bind the wires together. Otherwise…' Bryon froze and shook violently for a moment.

'Don't die on me here.'

'It's not going to happen.' Bryon wiped his hands and held them in front of the wires. 'Ethan? Get in the car.'

The thought of getting behind the wheel—the first time since the accident—knotted his stomach. As soon as he gripped the steering wheel, the crash played through his mind all over again.

He saw the reversing lights fast approaching them and the toddler in the rear window, staring, holding a doll. The driver was slumped between the front seats and there was nothing he could do about it.

Ethan couldn't hear Bryon repeatedly asking if he was ready.

As they slammed into the back of the car, the glass exploded, and the bonnet crunched up like a takeaway foil tray. Everything loose in the car slapped around and settled on the floor, until they were left with the sound of radiator water steaming over the hot engine. The car didn't have airbags and Heston didn't have his seat belt on. Ethan was uninjured, but Heston was left buckled up against the dashboard. In shock, in pain, but alive. The driver of the other car gurgled with the semi-conscious pain of a broken back. Luckily, the little girl ducked behind the rear seat which saved her life, the Ambulance crew told him later.

A loud knock on the window startled Ethan back to the moment.

'Are you ok?' Bryon asked.

He wound down the window and wiped his face. 'I'm ready. Let's go.' He took out his phone and set the stopwatch running.

'Kill the engine after three seconds,' Bryon stressed. 'No matter what.' He got into position with the wires in each hand.

Ethan gripped the key and watched for Bryon's signal.

'Ok, go!'

He turned the engine over and over, whilst Bryon bound together the exposed ends of the first pair of wires, then grabbed the second pair. Clock check: two seconds up. Bryon held the second pair of exposed wires over each other and pinched the ends. Three seconds were up. Ethan knew what he had to do, but Bryon wasn't done. No more than three, Bryon stressed. Three and a half seconds passed. It was too late already. Ethan released the key and looked over at Bryon. He twisted the wires together once and let them go just as the engine died. Everything fell quiet. *Had they done it?* Ethan wondered if there was a delay in the alarm going off until The Vkng's music cut through the night air.

'Perfect.' Bryon sat back onto his heels. 'We're good.'

'It went past three seconds.' Ethan sighed with relief and got out of the car. 'I was sure the alarm was going to cut in.'

'I told you three, but it was actually four seconds. I needed a buffer just in case you were sloppy.' Bryon shut the panel door and put his lock pick tool back in his wallet.

In a parallel universe somewhere, the alarm would have gone off, a high-pitch echo cut through the night air, as Bryon and Ethan ran from the compound, with police sirens in the distance. It was a good job Bryon was there. He could never have managed it by himself. Then a thought struck him. 'Why don't you have a key?'

'I quit this morning.' Bryon went around the back of the building and held the rear window open.

'We're breaking and entering?'

'Shut up and get in there.'

Ethan climbed up on to the windowsill and stepped through onto a backroom desk.

The port-a-cabin creaked as they walked through to El Gato's office. There, Bryon pulled the blinds down, flicked on the desk lamp, and started up the printer. He tucked in his Hawaiian shirt, lifted a set of keys from a cupboard, and removed a laptop from some drawers. A Pirelli Calendar on the wall had a photo of a bikini-clad, stiletto-wearing girl covered in oil leaning over a car engine, wiping imaginary sweat from her forehead. El Gato's taste for women froze time for March 1992 and turned the calendar into a permanent office fixture. A pair of the biggest bolt croppers Ethan had ever seen lay against the wall and took some effort to lift. Next to it was a long bar with a large screw thread point at one end which skewered a heavy sliding weight.

'What's this?'

'I don't know the name for it.' Bryon fed a sheet of paper under the scanner lid. 'But you wind that threaded spike into a lock and slam the weight into the opposite end of the bar until it rips the lock open.'

'Why would El Gato need it if he's the key holder?'

'Sometimes people ask him to do other jobs. Ones which don't go through the accounts.'

Ethan held the jaws of the bolt croppers up to eye level and squeezed the handles together. They felt so powerful and begged for something to cut. 'And these?' Ethan accidentally knocked the croppers against the floor hard enough to crack the partition flooring. 'Oops. Does El Gato even use them?'

'All the time. They're normally in the back of his van, but I guess they were needed today.'

'I need to cut something with these.'

'Can we just get this form stuff done and get out of here?' Bryon finished scanning the forms and Ethan helped him fill in the basic details. Though laborious, it didn't take too long with Bryon double-clicking and tabbing around the screen. Everything went well until the section titled, *Reasons to Enact*. They needed something beyond trespassing. Ethan wasn't the landowner or an affected resident either.

'What's your top ten reasons for hating gypsies?' Bryon asked.

'Easy: they're thieving scum.'

'Not sure that'll fly.'

'Thieving gypsy bastards?'

'I didn't mean make it sound better, I meant, use something else.'

'How about theft, nuisance, and assault?'

'Still no good. You don't have police reports for any of that, so it'll be treated as subjective misde-meanours or petty civil disorders. Think criminal, otherwise, nothing will happen. Try again.'

Bryon began Googling for ideas.

A town map on the wall had a list of potential new business sites marked out. The leisure centre had a red dot on it. 'You're bidding for the leisure centre contract? What are the chances of getting it?' Ethan asked.

'High. Hermanez has cut the costs to the bone. In fact, he's going to struggle to get anyone to work there.'

Ethan then thought about the bolt croppers again. 'How about if damage has been caused to the property?'

'That's criminal damage. I like it.'

'The entrance gates,' Ethan said.

'It might not be enough.' Bryon Googled for some more info. 'Are there more than six vehicles on site?'

'Yes.'

'Any abuse to the Owner or Agent?'

'Reed lives there, so he's the *Agent*, I guess. He'll vouch for us.'

'That's enough. Damage, abuse, and exceeding the vehicle threshold. A hat-trick.' Bryon got to work on the forms and left Ethan to nose around the desk opposite him. In a tray of paperwork, were various invoices and receipts, and one other which caught his eye. A sheet had been folded in two and placed on the top of the tray with the name Edwardo Hermanez written in Bryon's distinctive handwriting. Ethan opened it and read his resignation. It contained three short sentences: It thanked him for the opportunity to work, his wish to leave—effective immediately—and finally to wish

Hermanez all the best for the future. There was no reason to leave mentioned. Ethan folded it back up and held it under the desk out of view. Something made him question that directionless future. Bryon, ever the optimist, had nothing lined up, he just wanted out. But there was another thought. They'd just broken into the office. If El Gato never received the resignation, then technically they couldn't have broken in. Sure, they'd used an unconventional method to enter, but it wouldn't have been illegal. Ethan folded the paper into a quarter and placed it in his back pocket. It didn't feel wrong, and usually, his *Slings and Arrows* would make him suffer if it was a bad move.

He thumbed through a thick supplier catalogue of security equipment and found a big section devoted to Wi-Fi routers and Network connectivity.

'Is there a way of getting the Internet out into the leisure centre field?' Ethan held up the page from the catalogue.

'You'll have a few options: Satellite, mobile, or, hopping on an existing system if there's one in place. What are you thinking?'

'Just for filming. It'll be great to upload edits directly from the field. Could we install something and not tell anyone?'

'You'll need a power source.' Bryon switched on the printer and waited for it to settle. 'Satellite broadband is probably too much for what you need, so that leaves mobile. You could buy some access for the entire site.'

Buying a contract just to jump on some Wi-Fi occasionally was a bit heavy. 'Is there a way of getting it for free?' Ethan asked.

'No. Someone's got to pay for it somewhere.' He thought for a moment. 'Unless you scan the area, find out what signals are available, and then approach whoever owns them.'

'You think they'd share it?'

'Unlikely. Someone could hack the router. And before you ask, no I can't. Wait a minute, I remember seeing something which might do what you need.' Bryon brought up a website and turned the monitor around to Ethan. 'This is what you need.' On the screen was a BT advert for something called a *Shoebox* which offered an untethered long-range Wi-Fi, portable and personal. The website said *Users can connect via Bluetooth and get online within a fifty-metre range.*

'How much?'

'Cheap. £184.99'

'That's not cheap.'

'Maybe not.' Bryon went to Infinite Security's business account and logged into their supplier catalogue. 'The equipment order I placed this morning hasn't been processed yet. I'll just add another item for you and switch the delivery instructions to Depot collection.'

'You can do that?'

'I've already done it.' Bryon gave an order printout to Ethan. 'Just present this at the Depot address listed. It should be there by tomorrow afternoon.'

'Isn't El Gato going to notice?'

'Probably, but it'll take a while. Eventually, it'll either be cancelled or paid for. No biggie.'

Bryon also gathered all the council application printouts and stapled them together. 'There you go. That should do it. You do realise that moving gypsies is hard work, right? I mean, it'll be easier to get them to leave of their own accord, or befriend them so they don't bother you.'

'I don't think either of those options are going to work. I've met a few of them and they've already got it in for me.'

'You've got some time, though. It's got to be worth a try?'

'I'm going to try a few things, but this application is if all else fails.'

They left the office the same way they entered. Bryon removed the switch bypass from the alarm box, tidied up the cables and shut the panel door.

'Oh, one more thing,' Ethan remembered he had a photo of the dog tags on his phone. 'Reed has lost touch with his troop and the council claim he's not even military. Could you search for Lance

Corporal Joel Reed and see if these numbers match anything?'

Bryon zoomed into the photo and read the characters on the tags. 'Send that to me and I'll see what I can dig up.'

15

CARAVAN CHAOS

Sometimes taking a step forward hurts from carrying the weight of something wrong. It might manifest as pain, but it's most likely just a feeling. Ethan felt heavy this morning, yet he slept well for his final night on Heston's sofa, his cereal was still in date, and the coffee was hot enough to burn the roof of his mouth. Everything was as it should, except for a sluggish feeling, as if Flu was coming. He stepped off the bus outside the leisure centre and waited until it pulled away before walking across the flattened gates. Being filmed was the priority, however, despite many failed call attempts and unanswered messages, he had no idea if Dixel would show up again. The shape of the day just wasn't panning out and that heavy feeling just got worse once he'd walked around the corner of the main building.

A car had sliced through the hedge on the far side of the field and lay belly up, the windows were blown out, and kids were climbing all over it. The gypsy camp had doubled in size and the pool was getting a lot of attention. The rats ran around the edge with sticks in hand, wheelie-ing their bikes, and there was something else. That heaviness he carried didn't go away. It was like his shadow dug its fingertips into the earth to slow him down.

Between the car and the pool, some kids bickered over who should carry a red paint tub. Eventually, one kid hoisted it up onto his chest and walked it a dozen steps closer whilst his friend stood well clear. The kid placed the tub gently back on the floor. This thing was being handled like it was made of glass.

Reed's caravan had that locked look from a hundred metres away and something on the horizon blurred his view; the pool wasn't as crisp as it should have been. The bushy sunburnt-brown ground created a rough-edged woody feel to it. Something was very wrong. At around forty metres away, he finally realised the pool was full of pallets, wood, and other crap.

That heavy feeling cramped into a shit-fest on his intentions.

His Vans swelled with a planned kicking.

A queue of punches formed in his fists.

Kids bounced up and down on timber pieces

and ran across the top, hollering with play as some others tried to chase them off. This was no joke. A truck must have dropped a full load and it would take a miracle to clear it out.

'Who dumped all this in here?' Ethan shouted. He poked around beneath the top layer of wood and found an old wardrobe, some fruit packing crates, planks of wood, interior doors, skirting boards, and flattened cardboard boxes.

Could it have been Kirsty who ordered it filled? She did take an interest. It couldn't have been; local authorities don't act that fast. The thought only stung for a moment as Dixel arrived with a back-pack carrying too much equipment again. He'd normally make a quip, but she saw his face.

'What's up?' She noticed the pool, then the gravity of the day arrived. 'This is it? I thought you said it was rideable?'

'It *was* yesterday.'

'And I had to walk *all* the way here.' She put her heavy bag on the floor. 'I don't believe it.'

'I think we can clear this.' Ethan jumped onto the pallets and began throwing pieces of timber out onto the grass.

'You're joking? There's too much.' She went over to a few kids and asked them about the pool. They said they didn't know anything about it and were more interested in her bag.

'What's in this?' A young girl picked it up.

'That's mine,' Dixel said.

'Is it valuable?' Another girl was quick to join her friend. Ethan snatched the bag out of their hands. 'That's not for you.' He handed it back to Dixel who checked the zip.

As much as Ethan wanted all the little gits to find something else to do for the rest of the day, he needed more hands to help. Dixel offered a twenty-pound bribe, which caught their attention. Until they realised, she meant twenty total, not per person.

'£100,' a boy said and then he kept pushing the point again and again, as if his chances were increasing. He even got all puppy-dog cute about it too as his persistence shape-shifted to the pleasant desperation of a best-friend. It didn't work.

'We're screwed,' Dixel said.

The few pieces Ethan had cleared hadn't made a dent. 'That's the attitude.'

Dixel hoisted her bag on her back. 'I'm off unless you've got a better idea.'

'Of course.' He had nothing; just dead air surrounded by criminal records on BMX's.

'One that doesn't involve me breaking my back, I hope.' She sat back down on the ground and took a bite out of an apple.

· · ·

If you stand in the breeze long enough, something will blow your way. Ethan's dad used to say that whenever he needed money; and he always needed it. He could be smart for a drunk. Philosophy through a pint glass sounded like academic astrophysics to a ten-year-old and it took him a long time to figure out that the Breeze was metaphorical. It could have been anything, as the point was to deflect the conversation away from the bottle. The breeze he needed was a *good* idea. Ethan realised that *Ideas* arrived if only he silenced the dumb thoughts of *Wants* and *Needs*. The first few ideas he dismissed as they involved either tools he didn't have or hands he didn't want.

That wrecked car gave him *Ideas*. If he could get it to start and create a winch of some sort, he could yank those palettes out. A quick scavenge under the caravan resulted in what he needed: a couple of climbing ropes inside an old rucksack, that, when joined together, would reach the car with slack to spare. On the walk over to the car, he felt mighty proud of his idea-configuring. Even the climb through the window didn't slow his confidence; if Bryon could do it, surely, he could. He smashed the ignition casing off with a half brick, then stripped the two wires bare. The initial spark as they touched together proved the battery was still charged and that engine turned over. With a little push on the accelerator, the engine spun up into a steady heart-beat. He held a thumb up to Dixel and shouted, 'It's looking good!'

One of the front tyres had blown off, but the wheel hub was firmly in place. He tied one end of the rope around the hub then walked to the pool and tied the other end around a pallet. Back at the car he put it in gear and released the clutch. The wheel spun like crazy, yet instead of hoisting that pallet out the rope just slipped over the hub. The engine spluttered. He revved it some more and thick smoke plumed out the exhaust. That rope couldn't grip. He dropped down the revs and began the acceleration slowly. The rope snagged a few times as it looped around and it almost looked like it would catch on itself, but never did. The engine sputtered again and then died.

Someone had drained the tank.

On a defeated walk back to the pool, Dixel didn't have to ask how it went. The thought of grafting for the rest of the day to clear everything out was too painful to discuss. Calluses formed just thinking about it. He needed that breeze of ideas more than ever now.

'There's got to be another way.' The leisure centre buildings were designed for comfort and light entertainment. Nothing good for shifting debris out of a hole. Some industrial units beyond the perimeter fence could be helpful. An older kid finished carrying that tub near the pool, dropped it, and sloshed out some liquid. The kid was Darragh from the previous day.

'What are they doing?' Ethan asked.

'I don't know. I can't tell. Is that water?'

Then Ethan recognised the shape of the container. It wasn't a paint tub. It was a petrol can. The type that people carried in the back of their car ready for that one time when they may just break down. He looked over at the car on its roof: the boot was open, and the fuel cap was off. They had syphoned the tank. Before he could shout at the kids, Darragh struck the flint on his lighter and caught the fumes. A flame six feet high flashed the air, and the kids ran backwards shielding their faces. In the micro-seconds which followed the flame sunk into the pool and turned the whole thing into an inferno. All the other kids cheered and came over to watch as the smoke billowed into the sky.

The plume of smoke would be seen for miles. In the town people would wonder as to its source, as this wasn't just some back-garden bonfire, this was on an industrial scale. The flames popped and flicked, as some kids threw more debris onto it, then the wind lifted and dragged them even higher. That gypsy breeze had won against the guff of his weak ideas. Ethan sat, gripped some weeds, and yanked them out of the ground.

Dixel shielded her mouth with her t-shirt and

squinted into the heat. Flecks of smouldering embers jumped and swirled about in the air. She swore into her hand as a flame leapt up against the side of the caravan.

16

BATTLE AND RESCUE

Ethan ran towards the caravan before Dixel even had a chance to move. Within seconds the fire had engulfed the whole back wall. He squinted into the heat, grabbed a sheet of plywood, and threw it onto the side to smother the flames. It did little to quench the fire and just pushed the flames out towards his fingers.

He heard the dogs yelping inside.

They were trapped.

The caravan would not be able to withstand the heat for any more than a few minutes.

He had to act fast.

With one hard kick to the lock of the caravan door, it buckled. A second kick broke it away from its hinge and opened enough for him to push through.

The fire crept around to his side of the van.

Inside, there was a pinching stench of melting plastic and a layer of brown-grey smoke at head height, the heat had melted a large section of the plastic wall and fittings. The dogs jostled and jumped the edges of their basket in an attempt to free themselves, whilst the fibreglass back wall fizzed and crackled inches away from the bed. Everything around him was man-made and extremely flammable: acrylic, polyester, and plastic. Dixel couldn't see a thing through the smoke pumping out through the door until Ethan jumped through it with two puppies in his hands.

'Grab these.' He thrust them into her arms, then took a couple of big gulps of air and ran back inside. Less than ten seconds later, he returned with another pair. 'And these.'

'Wait How many more?'

'It's getting worse.'

He coughed and shot back into the room again.

Dixel carried the four wriggling pups out to the dirt and set them down on the floor. 'Someone keep an eye on these!' She shouted to the kids watching the pool fire. Ethan appeared in the doorway again and handed Dixel another pair of dogs. The air was almost unbearable inside and he needed a moment to wipe the stinging smoke from his eyes. He coughed and spat onto the floor. The caravan appeared to melt in front of them.

'It's ok,' Dixel said. 'They're all safe now.'

'There's two more.' He ran back inside one more time.

Dixel saw the rear corner collapse. 'Don't, you idiot.'

Ethan pushed through the smoke and heat one more time to the bedroom. The roof was burnt through, and droplets of plastic had already set the bed on fire. The last two puppies were limp as he scooped them out of the basket, but before he could run out through the door again, a large section of the ceiling fell and blocked the exit. He pushed into the tiny smoke-filled cubical toilet and slammed the door. It offered a little protection from the heat, but at least the ceiling was still in place. He put the dogs into the sink and ran cool water all over them then splashed water on his face and neck. The dogs sputtered into life, disorientated and whimpering for protection. The fire had already begun to warp the door. Through the small gap in the window, he managed to catch the attention of a girl who took the dogs from him. The relief was only momentary, as the searing heat melted the top of the door, allowing hot smoke to pour in. He got down on the floor to gulp in the last of the good air and watched the flames cover the ceiling. If he didn't get out of there in the next few seconds, molten plastic would fall and burn him alive.

Then he noticed metal rings in each corner the floor panel. He flicked up the loops and pulled on each until the panel released. Daylight broke through the ceiling and fiery blobs quickly threatened to drip. He flipped the panel above his head as a shield and felt a lump thud on its surface. Within a second he dropped through the floor to the dirt and rolled away from the access panel. Burning plastic soon broke through and landed on the ground. It felt as if the fire engulfed him from all sides. Once he spotted daylight, he scuffed along under the van on his elbows until Dixel helped him get to his feet and guided him away. At that moment a fire engine pulled up alongside them and officers jumped out of the cab. They rolled out the hose, connected it to the tank and a few seconds later water blasted all over the van whilst another team tackled the pool.

'Are the dogs all safe?' Ethan asked and looked back towards the patch of ground where the puppies lay.

'Yes, I've got them' she said.

Ethan checked the blanket. There was seven, he'd brought out eight. 'One's missing!'

The disorientated stray had crawled away from its spot and headed for the pool as if drawn by the heat. Its little legs powered towards the pool edge, bobbing, and weaving in distress with no sense of the danger.

Just one stray flame could engulf it.

17

REEDS MOTIVATION

Ethan ran over, skidded, and scooped the dog up into his chest, then rolled away from the flames into the black boots and florescent trousers of a fire officer.

'Let me take that little buddy from you.' The officer helped him away as another gave him some oxygen from a breathing apparatus.

Only one officer handled the caravan with a single hose. Its two remaining walls blew over from the force and the final flames were finished off with a hand-held fire extinguisher. A pathetic end to a feeble structure. The council car of Kirsty Sapsford pulled up beside the fire engine. Reed jumped out of the passenger seat, holding his head, shouting *No* over and over.

'What the hell happened?' Reed said. 'My stuff! The dogs!'

'They're safe.' Dixel pointed to them wrapped up on the blanket.

Ethan pulled the oxygen mask from his face, 'It was an accident.' He wasn't sure if *Accident* was the right word; fuel didn't appear out of thin air, and a pool full of pallets didn't either. The only true *accident* came from the flames which leapt onto the caravan. 'I couldn't save anything else.' A slew of pathetic apologies bulged tight in his throat and would have tumbled out if it weren't swollen with guilt.

The flames of the pool fire still raged and snorted like a dragon, despite three men working on it. Once the pool was under control, Kirsty felt comfortable approaching the officer in charge.

'We'll need to make this area safe,' she said. 'Is there anything you can do until we can get a team out here and close this off?'

'We could run a clearing exercise if the rest of the lads are OK with it.' A few of them confirmed they could stay on. 'We can treat this as training.' He tipped his hat like a cowboy, then continued packing a hose into the appliance. Kirsty thanked them all and made a call back to the council. Two of the men removed a generator and some additional equipment, whilst the remaining officers got into the cab and made their way back to the station.

Reed walked through the ashen remains of the

caravan, picking at his possessions with a knife and throwing anything worth saving out onto the dirt.

'What's going to happen to the pool now?' Ethan asked Kirsty.

'A team will be despatched as soon as possible to fill the site.'

'You can't fill it in.' The greatest local skate discovery of the last decade began to rapidly slip away from him.

'I'm sorry, but we have to. This isn't safe. Someone could get seriously hurt.'

Some selfish grovelling would fix this.

'Don't ruin it for everyone. It's been here long enough without any problems.'

'This is a private site,' she said, then, 'Look, I know you want to ride here, but I can't leave it. The street services team will be here by this time tomorrow. I suggest whatever you want to do, you do it quickly.'

This was the break he needed. It was one of the shittiest ever, but he'd take it never-the-less.

Kirsty approached Reed tentatively. 'This may not be the best timing, but I have to either release that flat or hold it in your name. I strongly urge you to take it up. Whether you like it or not,' she paused, 'you're as good as homeless now.'

'Just take the damn flat,' Ethan said. Kirsty gave him a glare, but it wasn't as if her efforts had done any better. Only an idiot wouldn't take it. He'd give his right arm to have a place of his own.

A plastic car with multi-coloured panels bounced across the dirt and stopped by them. It was a woman from *Sweet Shelter Animal Rescue*. She radiated happiness in a pair of Mario Bros dungarees, oblivious to the sombre faces of the moment. Kirsty shook her hand and thanked her for coming out at short notice. Reed handed over the pup blanket. She promised him they'd get the best care and that he'd be welcome to visit at any time. The woman was also happy to give Dixel a lift back into town. Once the car had hummed off into the distance, all attention turned back to Reed. It was as if a huge cloud of *What next?* sat over him. Those pups being taken away whacked a big nail in the coffin of his purpose. There was literally no life left in his fight.

'Ok. I'll take it,' he said.

Kirsty's shoulders dropped as if a mountain of paperwork had been removed. 'It's the right decision,' she said and got back on the phone to reserve the property. After she had finished, she promised to return with the keys and visit the housing foundation shop to pick up some furniture. 'These circumstances will mean you'll get full emergency relocation support,' she said in a sweaty huff of successful breath. She slumped back down behind the steering wheel, gave a limp wave goodbye, and drove off the site.

'Flat life will be good for you,' Ethan said. 'A five-star hotel compared…'

'I know.' Reed picked up a shovel from underneath the caravan's remains and used it to scrape back the floor. Beneath the debris of a bench was a metal box. He unlocked it and lifted out some papers and six photographs. 'The important things are safe,' he said.

'Who are those people?' Ethan asked.

Reed checked the edges for burn marks. 'They're my troop.'

The photo of seven men in military uniforms was gathered around a Land Rover with a beach and palm trees behind them. Second from the left was a clean-shaven and tanned Reed, holding a hat up in the air, squinting into the sun, and cheering with the others.

The old dog. Kirsty was wrong. *Reed was Military, after all.* 'Kirsty said that they were all in your head.'

'Convenient for them.' He gathered up the photos and placed them back in the box then took out a folded piece of paper with a military stamp on it. 'This document proves the MOD owns this land and ownership *only* completes once the last serviceman has left. If they see me as unfit, or mentally unstable, they can get me out of here, but otherwise, I have every right to stay.'

'So, you're in active service?'

'Call it whatever you want, but I call it a technicality that a date wasn't added to the documents. I'm still on the MOD records, so, I appear to be the *hole* in the legal loophole. Or at least, was. Once I leave the land goes to the council and they do what they want with it.'

As Reed wandered throughout his ruined home, Ethan tried to feel for him, for everything lost, but it was hard. *Apologies* weren't what he needed. He would have seen and dealt with much more than this whilst in service. The Four Horseman of Kirsty's Pool Apocalypse were already on standby to fill it in, so the clock was ticking.

'But you gave me a therapist's card,' Ethan said. 'That means you're a bit nuts, right?'

'I'm not unstable. Loretta has been helping me with managing my PTSD.' He pulled a plastic container of pills out of his pocket. 'I just need a couple of these if things get too heavy.'

'Look at those feckin' druggies,' Darragh shouted over at them. 'Told you not to come back around here. This is our place now!'

'What's their problem?' Reed said.

Ethan scratched the back of his head and realised that no-one had told him. 'They started the fire.'

Reed did some hard maths and watched the boys on their bikes circling around laughing.

'I think they've got it in for me,' Ethan added.

Reed began tapping his hand on the pocket

with his knife in. Clearly agitated, he took a deep breath before he spoke. 'That's the last favour I do for them. I fixed their vehicle on the road a few days ago. I've met their parents. I thought they were okay with me.'

Darragh lifted a middle finger at them both and cycled off across the field back to the camp.

Reed slapped his hand over his mouth and dragged it down his stubble, then popped the lid off his medicine bottle and swallowed a couple of them. 'I'll string 'em up.'

The moment got lumpy under the tension, and Ethan tried to push a joke through the eye of a needle. 'If you're stringing them up, they deserve your best fishing line!'

Eye contact or a smile would have been nice, but Reed couldn't turn his head with all those neck muscles tightening. The pool looked like a blackened hole or the inside of a council estate dustbin after Halloween.

Reed joined him in the shallow end and inspected the surface. 'I think it's going to be OK.' He ran his fingers through the soot. 'Come back tomorrow and I'll have swept it by then.'

'You think it'll be good enough to skate?'

'We'll see,' he said.

'I'll stay and help.'

'I don't want you here. I need a distraction before I kill someone. Go. I've got a lot to do.'

Those pills appeared to have a fast-acting effect on his mood. No thanks for saving his animals or giving up the info about the arsonists. Just a big fat goodbye. Ethan was no stranger to hard work if it meant he got a skate out of it, but he also didn't have any intention of helping a grumpy stubborn sod, if he wasn't needed.

It wasn't until he was halfway across the field that he heard Reed swear into the direction of the gypsy camp. The man sure had his demons.

18

FILMING ATTEMPT

The following morning outside the leisure centre, Ethan found a gap in the hedge and saw more gypsy caravans had gathered overnight. A marquee had gone up for some kind of party. People had strung up bunting between their trailer homes and the horses were adorned in colours of pink and gold. Without Reed's caravan as an indicator, it wasn't even clear where the pool lay, initially.

Dixel tapped on Ethan's shoulder and startled him. 'What's going on?' she said through a mouthful of breakfast bar. It looked homemade.

'I can't believe it,' he said. 'It's packed out there.' The cars had ribbons tied across their bonnets and a horse and cart was dressed all fancy with flowers and streamers. People heaved bales of hay out of a 4x4 into the marquee. 'We've got to get it done though, so here's the plan.'

Dixel squatted down next to him and braced herself for maximum engagement.

'We get in the pool, film as much as we can, and get out.'

'You plan with all the precision of an amoeba,' she said.

'You over complicate things.'

A few men stood between some trailers talking whilst pop music played through a speaker system.

'It sounds like you're going to be skating to Keisha or Taylor Swift or whatever that is,' Dixel said. 'Don't look so miserable. I'll find a remix which matches to take the sting out of it.'

He couldn't tell if she was serious.

'Lighten up.' She slapped him on the back. 'It'll be amazing.'

He still couldn't tell.

They both pushed through the hedge and began walking across the field until the marquee blocked the gypsies' line of sight. From that point on, they ran as fast as they could towards the pool and jumped down inside it. The devastation from yesterday's raging inferno was barely noticeable apart from some soot dust in the tile grooves. Reed must have cleaned it with a power-washer. Crappy music floated over their heads which reminded Ethan of a bigger problem: that gap in the vehicles funnelled a steady stream of people in their direction.

'Problem.' Ethan watched the partygoers. 'I'm going to be on the coping a lot. It's too exposed.'

Many trailer windows faced them and for all he knew each window could have someone behind the nets staring straight back at him.

'Just don't go out the top.'

'I have to, otherwise, no-one will watch it.'

'And there's no point doing it unless your ego is being stroked, right?'

'Wrong.' Ethan felt attacked. She'd been working late, missing their meet-ups, kissing ass for the new boss. Skating was his domain, and she needed to stay the hell out of it. 'Yes, I'm here for the hits, but only so I don't get fired.' He didn't want to admit that he needed to cling on to the dying embers of his skate career. 'Also, Heston needs me on this.'

'Why? He's doing alright on his own. He's working, earning, driving, and has a social life— which is more than you have. And now he's about to get paid soon, so what exactly are you doing for him?'

'We're family!' Then, 'You don't know the half of it.'

'Please, elaborate.'

Ethan stewed on his thoughts for a moment. Dixel sure knew how to cut an argument in half and slice the fat off it. Which was easy to do when Daddy was at home making breakfast bars, and

Mummy is topping up the bank account with her top job.

'It's not about me,' he said, 'but I, we, can't produce a crappy edit. It doesn't matter how great you are at your job, if you don't have any good footage to work with, the edit will suck. That's how it works. You'll have to trust me. I'll be on the coping a lot, so I need to stop these idiots from seeing me.'

'Alright. Stop bunching up your knickers. You'll pop a vein.' She took a seat on the transition and prompted him for one of his bright ideas.

'I'll be back in a moment.' He climbed out over the top, ran to a pallet by a bush, and dragged it back towards the lip. He then quickly retrieved a panel of plywood and climbed back down into the pool. 'I'm going to make a barrier and need something heavy to prop this stuff up against.'

An oil drum alongside one of the trailers looked perfect. The curtains weren't twitching and no amount of watching would predict the future, so he seized his opportunity. He sprinted low and exposed like grouse during shooting season until he reached the barrel and found it full of water. It weighed a tonne. He was sure he could tip it, but the thud alone could attract a lot of attention. It was good but hard work. He got down on the ground and looked under the trailer for a better option. There didn't seem to be any movement, so he crawled through to the other side whilst footsteps thudded above, and voices shouted. The argument appeared to be about the ridiculous size of a wedding dress. The bride argued she could break her neck on the train. A woman shouted back that it was *traditional*, and her grandmother would turn in her grave.

'She had eight brothers and sisters,' the bride said. 'There's no room to turn in that grave!'

Ethan stifled a laugh and kept crawling.

The steps by the front door were clear, but to the right, a large snarling Alsatian dog stared at him from its bed.

He froze. *Does no-one like cats?* Within two heart beats the dog leapt up and ran towards him, barking.

He ducked back under the van and rolled into the centre. The sparkling chime of a chain pulling through a peg in the ground yanked the dog to a halt just inches away. It snapped and snarled at the intruder.

The trailer door flew open, and an irritated woman shouted, 'What are you barking at?'

Another younger female shouted, 'He's probably chasing rats again. Just give him some chicken.'

A bony carcass landed on the floor, the dog snatched it up and carried it back to its bed. The woman slammed the door and went back to her argument.

The motivation to find better pallet stacking

options rapidly faded as it wouldn't take long for the dog to crunch through those bones. Ethan returned to the other side of the caravan where, on a second viewing, the barrel looked twice as heavy. He briefly stared at his wobbly reflection, then glanced through the window beside him. Nancy, the girl from a couple of days ago, stood in a full wedding dress. She spotted him, smiled, waved, then motioned to her friend to look at the gormless lump watching them. They both laughed, whilst the older woman tacked pins into the back of the dress, oblivious.

He dropped down from view and squatted next to the barrel. This was almost as bad as the dog chasing him. The next ten seconds felt like sixty whilst he waited for someone to burst out of the trailer and chase him off. He knew he couldn't wait to be caught. He gripped the edge of the barrel and pushed it with all his weight. The first couple of inches off the ground were easy but the rest of the angle was a dead weight to lift. He almost lost his grip, his arms buckled at the elbows, and he used his chest against the side to tip it the rest of the way. When it thudded on the ground, the water spread out like a huge jellyfish and seeped into the cracked earth. He rolled it towards the pool with growing speed, until he realised it was turning to the right and would miss the pool by a mile. He heaved the rim straight and kept rolling, but it seemed the faster he rolled it, the more the barrel wanted to turn away from its target. Eventually, he gave up and dragged it by the rim to the edge of the pool.

Ethan paced around catching his breath. 'Someone spotted me. A girl from yesterday.'

'So, what's the problem?' Dixel peered out over the top. 'No-one's coming.'

'They might, though,' he said. 'I have a feeling I flirted with someone's fiancé.'

'You said you didn't know why they torched the pool!'

'I didn't know she was getting married,' he said. 'Besides, blame isn't helping right now.' Ethan looked out over the coping for signs of an angry mob raging towards them. It appeared clear, so he got up, moved the barrel, leant the ply against it, positioned the pallet, and jumped back into the pool again. 'That should work.' Then, 'Okay. It looks like we can actually film something.'

Dixel unpacked her camera and positioned a couple of GoPro's: one faced the deep end and the other faced the steps. Finally, she placed a Canon on a tripod right in the middle of the pool.

'Not there,' Ethan said. 'I'll run into it.'

'Don't worry, I'll be changing the angles, but I need to see what you're doing first.'

He got up on the lip behind the ply barrier. 'I think you should just capture everything. We might not have time for me to warm up.'

'I'm already recording.'

Ethan dropped in and took his first figure-of-eight line behind Dixel, up over the steps, then back down towards the deep end. He knew he needed to establish his ability to carve the pool first and kept his line low and fast, feeling the pump all the way around, and back out again. His return had enough speed to smith grind the coping for three or four blocks, double back on himself to catch a little backside tailslide, then hit a few more blocks for a 5-0. The next line went frontside around the steps and back into the deep for a frontside alley-oop to 5-0 for a couple of blocks, before allowing himself to fall back into the transition. The next drop into the deep was a fast frontside tailslide, the next, a backside crailslide. He knew he hadn't warmed up properly yet, but his adrenaline surged and made up for it. With the next pump, he aimed for that damned frontside ollie. This time he was ready for the curved coping and ollied well clear of the lip. It was a relief to hear his wheels land on the concrete and pump back through the transition again. After that move, he ended his run and pulled up just beside Dixel.

'That was great. I got it all.' She grabbed the camera from the shallow, placed it in the middle of the deep end flat bottom, then ran up to the coping to catch Ethan's backside tricks. 'Ok, I'm set. Go again.'

'Hang on.' He was still panting on the flat.

'I thought you were an athlete?' She laughed and framed the shot through the viewfinder.

After a minute he rolled back down into the pool from the shallow end and built on his last run, without all the pumping. He wanted to get into *his* comfort zone: a feeble grind, a body-jar, a frontside lipslide, a couple more frontside and backside ollies, and one with a tail-smack on the way in. Mostly by accident, but it counted. He felt good and wanted Reed to make an appearance and see how he was doing. The practise had paid off. The pool felt much faster and easier to ride than before, to the point where he stopped worrying about the sudden change of transitions. Just the simple change of lifting his head higher to see through the line instead of focusing on what was immediately ahead of him was worth it alone. He felt like he now had the *key*. He wished someone had taught him that technique years ago, maybe he wouldn't have been such an embarrassment over the years. Dixel switched her camera angles once again and they shot another couple of lines. He paused in an axle stall on the coping. 'Have you had enough yet?'

'Me? No. You're the one who looks like a sweaty cricket ball. Is that all you've got?'

It got to the point where he was running out of tricks. His ramp skills were reasonable, but any fool could see that he was limited. He'd either need to go higher or faster or both to compensate. It was time to throw something big together; he needed a big trick: that Invert Reed showed him was etched into his mind. It was old-school, but retro-cool too. He'd dreamt about it so many times it felt like he could do it already.

19

SPARKLE MOTION

'I'm going to try something new. I might not make it.'

'Sounds great already.' Dixel set up her camera based on Ethan's instruction for the angle. She still hated him telling her what to do but couldn't be bothered to argue with him.

He pumped around the shallow, rode up the deep end, planted his hand on the coping and launched himself upside down. He missed the grab completely and the board shot up into the air. He ran down the transition with his hands covering his head, but the front truck knocked him to the floor.

'You, OK?' Dixel shouted. A lump formed on his head and then he saw the blood on his hand. He laid down again and let the flecks of light disappear from his vision.

'That looked amazing.' Dixel joined him on the

flat bottom. 'Are you ok? Are you going to be able to try it again?'

Ethan held his head with his hand and sat up again. The blood on his hand was worse, but Dixel reassured him it wasn't too bad. Then a line of blood trickled across his head towards his ear.

'I take that back. You look a mess. You shouldn't try it again.'

'I've got to. I need something to end on.'

The slam was unfortunate, but a freak accident. The first attempt was always the worst, and he knew he had to get back on it before the fear set in. Dixel thought he was an idiot again, but she always over-reacted to a little blood. His second attempt fared much better: he planted his hand, caught hold of the board, but the stall was too much. His weight was too far over the coping and landed on the top. The third attempt was better. He got the balance right his time, and pulled the board into the transition, only to slip off the back onto his ass.

'I've got this next one,' he said.

The blood on his head had streaked lines across his scalp with the momentum, but at least it had congealed enough to stay out of his eyes. Not only that but time was running out, as more gypsies were arriving for the event. With his energy sapped, he dropped in again and completed a figure-of-eight back into the deep end. He planted his hand, smacked his tail, caught the board, and pulled it back in. The next thing he realised he was riding along the flat, stoked, and relieved.

'You get that?'

'I got it,' she said.

Thank God.

They both sat in the middle of the pool and watched the camera playback. The footage looked good. He could hardly believe the person blasting around the bowl was himself. He covered his mouth so Dixel wouldn't see his jaw drop.

'I'm happy,' he said.

'Shall I edit in those bails, too?'

'No. Use the slams only.' The cut on his head ached more now he'd stopped riding. He poured a little water on it and wiped the blood with some tissues. In the quiet moments that followed he asked why Dixel hadn't been so committed to filming recently. She gave one of those looks that made him feel like he was the problem. He hated those.

Dixel packed away a camera. 'Work is important to me.'

Priorities, he thought.

'The old HR team are gone,' Dixel said. 'Things are edgy at work.' She told him Blacker had pulled in a new Human Resources team. As far as Ethan was concerned, HR was the most pointless entity in any company. When a company got to a size that it needed to employ a team of people to manage the people, something was definitely broken.

Then Dixel had a thought that hurt, 'Why can't you call someone else up? Why do you need me all the time?' she said. And when Ethan failed to respond, she spelt out the trouble in short painful stabs like a phonetic tattoo. 'You need to sort out your friendships.'

He took a long slug on a bottle of water and searched for a reason. He settled for a shrug. She had a habit of picking at his wounds. He was sure she'd see it another way, like she was helping, or something, but people don't talk about things for a reason. Sit in his shoes for a day and she'd button up her wide opinions fast.

'Heston is on a training workshop in London,' Ethan said.

'He's not. I saw him this morning.'

'He left on Tuesday. Suitcase and everything.'

'Unless he has a twin, he was in work, because I saw him,' she said.

With so many days and nights jammed in front of the editing suite, Dixel sure got her dates mashed. There were no messages on his phone. Loyalties were family deep first. Everyone else came second. Unless, of course, that new girlfriend put a spanner in Heston's plan. That would probably be it. Nothing upsets the schedule like a good female.

The only medicinal cure for a pool closing in on

him was a quick dose of horizon, distance, and background. He sat on the coping in the spot behind the barrier. The chorus of Queens, *We Will Rock You*, floated through the air, fading in and out like a drowsy sleep. A cheap tiara glinted on the head of a girl walking towards them.

It was Nancy.

He almost didn't recognise her until she swept a delicate veil from a bridal headpiece clear of her face. She had bright red lipstick, heavy mascara, and a thick spread of foundation like the mud on the sides of her trainers.

'What you doing?' She spoke as if it was completely normal to be walking around dressed for a wedding.

'Get down into the pool,' Ethan said. 'Does anyone know you're here?'

'No.' She hooked the veil back behind her head. 'They're all too busy with themselves to notice me.'

You're the bride, Ethan thought. *How can you not be missed?* 'Dixel. This is Nancy.'

'Everyone calls me Nan,' she said through her chewing gum.

'Great.' Dixel kept her smile up like a draw-bridge and looked at Ethan. 'So?'

'She's cool,' he said. 'It's the others I'm worried about.'

'I'm beginning to think you're stupid,' Nancy said. 'You must have some balls to come back here.

Darragh was proper livid. He couldn't stop talking about fighting you yesterday.'

'I'm not going to fight a kid.'

'He's fourteen, but just looks twelve. It's the others who'll make a mess of you.'

'Why didn't you say you were getting married?' Ethan said. 'I can see why the others didn't want me talking to you. Slightly protective, aren't they?'

'I'm a catch,' she winked. 'Yeah, well, this… ' she pointed to her made-up face, 'I've got to go through with it. My fiancé is dog-shit, but there's nothing I can do about it.'

'This is an arranged marriage?' Dixel asked.

'For now.' She reached out for Ethan's shoulder to stabilise herself as she stepped onto his board. 'Until I un-arrange it later. Give us a push, will you?'

Suddenly a squeaky pre-pubescent voice shouted her name, 'Get out of there, Nan!' All four foot eight of Darragh was standing at the coping and swearing that he'd warned Ethan enough.

'Go back home,' Nancy shouted. 'He's like CCTV on legs, I swear.'

Darragh pointed a finger of death at Ethan and ran back towards the marquee.

'I think we're done, Dixel. Time to leave.'

'Ignore him.' Nancy urged Ethan to push her around on the board. Dixel collapsed her tripod and stuffed it into a bag. A gang of four older boys ran with Darragh across the field with bats and bars in hand.

'Jesus, Ethan. You better go now,' she said.

'They're only playing,' Nancy shouted as he sprinted off towards the leisure centre. 'What about your board?'

'Hang on to it for me,' he shouted back.

20

ABORT!

If he could make it to the leisure centre, he'd have a chance of losing them in the maze of walls. They gained a little ground on him, but that's what comes of a diet of cigarettes, cheap food, and the metabolism of a ten-year-old. Whilst Ethan lumbered across the field feeling each breast bounce like a flabby burger, the air slip-streamed through their legs without an ounce of body fat.

One of the good runners seemed to be made of legs. He was all up on Ethan's tailwind, but without backup, the kid had his brakes on. The next kid back was a snappy little Terrier with a mullet, a t-shirt tan, and legs that blurred like a cartoon. The next kid was a Boulder, who pounded along with bewildered, lethargic ease like he wasn't sure why he was chasing someone. The fourth kid looked the oldest, was smartly dressed, and used a half pot of hair gel to limit his wind resistance. The last dog in the fight was Darragh, many paces behind playing catchup and still sucking on a cigarette from the corner of his mouth.

Ethan reached the first building and needed a plan; to gain some distance or get out of the complex. He wished the kids came with IDs, as it would be nice to know if he could batter any of them without getting into trouble with the police.

He sprinted around the walls, down the corridors, and out across courtyards. The slaps of their feet echoed across the tiles like a round of applause at an afternoon's Cricket match. He ducked into a doorway and watched them all run past him. He had given them the slip, for now, but they'd soon realise and search every spot. The Lido had limited exits and only offered changing rooms to hide in. The kids would head straight for it. Instead, he headed downstairs into the darkness and found a spot with a view of the stairs.

One of the kid's trainers squeaked through the reception door.

'We know you're in here!' a small voice cried.

'Yeah, and we're going to rip you open!' the older kid shouted, and then began a cautious walk down the steps. Ethan was already used to the dark and had the advantage. He got to the back wall and rested against it. In the dark, accidents can happen; witnesses can't be sure, a fall can be a push, and no-one can prove otherwise—even a direct smack in the mouth can be denied. The boy stumbled around, hands outstretched, swearing he was going to slap Ethan. He spoke with all the confidence of a UFC champion with a backup entourage. Ethan watched the silhouette bumble around, reaching for the walls, sweeping low with his arms, and pushing and bumping around.

There was a sudden whoosh of nylon cutting through the stale air, and a faint line of light flashed across the boy's chest. It hauled him straight up and thudded his head into the ceiling. The room fell silent. Ethan pulled a tarpaulin sheet from a window and saw the unconscious boy swinging from the ceiling just a few feet from the floor. The rope around his chest went up to a pulley and back to a cement-filled counterweight on the other side of the room. The kid snoozed like a new-born.

He'd seen the same design in Reed's notepad: *The Strangle*.

Each element of the trap had no excess, no slack, no waste. It was fast, efficient, and perfectly designed. The best way to describe it was *professional*. Despite being made from found materials. Ethan couldn't guess which animal it would be effective for trapping. Bears didn't roam the streets. At the bottom of the stairs, there was a blue dot sprayed on the wall with an arrow coming out of it. The paint was fresh. Reed must have laid traps around the site, knowing the leisure centre would be the only place to hide.

'Thank you, Reed. Let's see what else you've got.'

Ethan ran to the top of the stairs and listened for signs of movement. Eventually, the older boy spotted him and shouted for his friends to follow. Ethan shot back down the stairs with the boy just metres behind. By the time he reached the next room, he saw another symbol on the wall: a blue dot with a left arrow. He kept to the left of the room and got to the back wall just as the lad got to the door.

Ethan kicked some boxes in the darkness to be sure the boy walked through the middle of the room, and his prey took the bait perfectly. With each step, he expected something to happen, but the boy came closer and closer until he could almost reach out and thump him. There was every chance that the room wasn't set, or the trap had been sprung already. When the kid got too close, Ethan pushed him back, and he staggered then tripped over something. A heavy rumble sounded and dozen huge plastic water barrels tumbled towards them both. Ethan dived out of the way, as the first few barrels knocked the lad across the room and the others pummelled him into a dazed and groaning mess on the floor.

The Mangle. Ethan smiled. *Two down and thank you, Reed.*

The third boy, the Terrier, kicked his way through the boxes and papers strewn about the floor, fumbling around in the dark. Ethan saw him coming and managed to get out of the second room and move further down the corridor. The next room he came too had a blue dot with a right arrow. He remembered Reed saying the deeper into the building, the prey got the more advanced the traps. It was the perfect justice he needed, and a shame Reed couldn't be there to watch it all unfold. Ethan hugged the right side of the wall, then found a tin can and threw it out into the corridor to lure the boy in his direction. The Terrier stood in the doorway, hesitated, then turned to leave, but was joined by the lethargic Boulder. The Terrier pushed the bigger boy in.

'You check it,' he said.

'Why me?' The Boulder tried to leave but the little kid pushed him back in.

Ethan watched the lump walk cautiously through the room. He bumped into a disused chair, stumbled a little and told his friend he was **OK**, then silently vanished. A voice of confused panic rose out of the ground and increased with volume and frequency as fear set in.

'What's happened?' The Terrier considered stepping into the room but didn't.

'I'm stuck,' the boy said. 'I can't move. Get me out.'

The Tangle, Ethan thought. The very trap he had fallen into when he first met Reed.

Eventually, the Terrier edged his way into the room towards his friend and felt the edge of the plunge pool. He could just about make out his friend, facedown, tangled in fishing wire, struggling to free himself.

Ethan couldn't allow the boy enough time to release his friend and crept around the edge of the room to the door. 'Come on then big man,' he shouted. 'Or are you going to pussy out too?'

The Terrier clattered out of the room swearing in a barely legible Irish accent. By the time Ethan settled in the back of the next room, the boy stood cautiously in the doorway. He saw what had happened to his friends and couldn't bring himself to race into another trap. He shouted for Darragh, and when he didn't get a response, he knew he was on his own. The Terrier edged forward waving his hands high in case something swung for his head. Little did he know Reed had laid a tripwire and the boy walked straight into it. By the time the lad felt it a rope had pulled tight around his legs, flipped him upside down, and left him swinging in the centre of the room.

The Dangle.

The kid thrashed around in a vulnerable panic

and tried to reach his ankles but couldn't. As much as Ethan wanted to cherish the moment he had to get to the next room as there was one last brat to deal with: Darragh.

'C'mon then!' Ethan's voice echoed through the hallway. The patter of tiny gypsy feet in cheap knock-off trainers slapped down the stairs. Darragh hesitated in the shaft of light at the end of the room. He pointed his dirty fag-stained finger, flicked away the cigarette, and swore he was going to pound Ethan's head in.

The mountain of crap on the floor held up his sprint. No-one went this deep, no-one felt it was worth it. It worried him that Reed hadn't gone this deep either. What prey would struggle through broken pallets, storage boxes, disused shelving units, discarded lockers, and old clothing rails? He tripped and stumbled then got to his feet again and kept pushing on. He heard Darragh behind, rabid and vicious with his threats and promises. No-one could be afraid of this kid. At best he was annoyingly persistent, at worst, he was a scrappy slapper with hepatitis spit.

He paused briefly to read the blue spray marking on the wall before entering the pitch-black room. A grid of nine dots. He hadn't seen that diagram in Reed's book. The arrow pointed left, so he trusted the plan and stuck close to the wall.

'You's bastard.' Darragh's voice echoed into the

empty darkness. 'I'm gunna slap you down, pick you up, and slap you down again.' He walked into the middle of the room, charged and tense from his adrenaline intentions, yet breathlessly tired from the chase too. He didn't even stop to wonder why the acoustics changed. There was an almost unbearable tension in Ethan's fingertips. He wanted that familiar click or tug of a pin to come quickly and get this over with. Darragh walked further. Ethan edged around the room to keep Darragh's framed silhouette in the faint light of the doorway. The room almost creaked with patience.

C'mon. Just a little more.

A sudden spark and flame of Darragh's lighter filled the room with a soft amber glow. Darragh spotted Ethan against the wall and jabbed his penknife out at him.

Behind the boy was Reed's trap.

A wall-mounted grid of sharpened fence posts. Painstakingly hoisted onto a frame and bound with rope, perfectly counter-balanced with a pulley system across the ceiling and attached to drums on the opposite wall. It must have weighed a tonne and taken a day to assemble. If the other traps were designed to catch a small animal, this one, was on another level. The force would kill instantly. For a moment, Ethan wondered what the loss would be to the world if this one kid vanished from the earth until the seriousness hit him: the kid could die, right now, in front of him.

He had to do something quickly.

'Don't move!' he shouted. 'There's a trap!'

'Too right, there is,' Darragh said. 'You're gunna be squealing like a little fat pig in a minute.'

'This place is rigged.' Ethan held his hands up and began to walk forward. 'Yes, you can gut the hell out of me, but don't move.' A tripwire cut across the floor in the light of the flame millimetres from Darragh's feet. He grinned as if he'd just pulled off some amazing feat of brains over brawn. The straining weapon of spikes to the right of him didn't relax. It only had one thing to do, and it silently waited for the wrong move. Once Ethan got within stabbing distance of Darragh's pathetic penknife, he knew he couldn't wait any longer. He grabbed the boy's wrist and pushed him back into the floor. The straining weights dropped, the pulley of ropes slapped against the ceiling, something stationary released its energy, and the hurtling brush of heavy wood whistled past them and slammed into the window. It punctured nine perfect holes the size of saucers into four-millimetre sheet steel on the window. As the contraption fell to the floor daylight flooded the room.

The rat under Ethan's weight fought to get to his feet and there wasn't enough relief to hold him down any longer.

'You tried to kill me!' He went for his penknife, but Ethan blocked him with his foot.

'You still want to fight? I just stopped you from being killed, you moron.'

Darragh's penknife tinkled like a spoon on the floor when he saw the fence post spikes strapped to the pallet. Stuttering bursts of empty venom stalled in his gut, his knees quivered, his hands trembled. The kid was determined to stay angry as his body sucked the blood from his legs and arms to protect the vital organs. 'You's…' His eyes backflipped in his skull and he slumped to the floor.

It wouldn't take long for Darragh to wake, and he didn't want to hang around to have another lame exchange. Darragh would eventually realise what had happened after seeing that massive device again. He might even consider thanking someone. Fat chance.

On the walkout, through the lower level, Ethan checked on the others. Everyone had released themselves from their traps and gathered in the room with the kid dangling upside down from the ceiling. Without their little mouthy runt of a leader, they had nothing to say to Ethan. They didn't even ask what happened to him, instead, they wobbled on plastic crates to untie their friend's legs.

Back upstairs, the sudden rush of daylight

agitated enough blood cells to think straight. Reed had gone too far. Kirsty said he wasn't all there and only a crazy would build something so dangerous. Reed knew he would run for cover in the building. It could have easily been him who got caught up in the traps. It didn't matter that Reed hadn't warned him of the danger.

Someone could have died.

Maybe Reed wasn't worth the effort after all.

21

DAY ZERO

The walk through the high street reminded Ethan how he hated mornings. Despite a fine grain sandpaper air grazing his skin, and a blue filter of daylight coating the buildings, it was still too early. A therapeutic lie-in couldn't be beaten, and it was critical recovery time for a skateboarder who killed it from tea-time to twilight. It's one of the things Ethan enjoyed about the N27 job: flexitime. Let the salarymen keep their premium rate rush hour. He had his own headache, but even Flint couldn't override a company policy. Flexitime was a big *screw you* to any company who believed regimented hours brought with it a happy employee. Some of the staff even gave it up and worked all the hours available in some kind of team-player act of loyalty. No thank you. Ethan didn't need Dennis to tell him a second time that he couldn't sleep on the reception sofa past 7 am as staff would be arriving. God forbid that anyone thought he chose to be there that early. He was up and out of the building well before seven.

The Coffee House was open, and Ethan waited outside on wet seats for Amit to deliver a brew as black as death and as hot as hell. Despite trying to carry the cup carefully out to the table, Amit spilt plenty with the agitation of fresh news. Thinking that he cared to know, Ethan explained why he was out so early.

'Heston's girlfriend is moving in—I had to be out last night.'

Amit brushed the comment away and flicked a tea towel at a nearby pigeon scavenging for crumbs. He couldn't wait to report on the police raid from the leisure centre as the camp size doubled overnight. Fearing an increase in Koi Carp thefts, the residents speed dialled complaints into the early hours until the police arrived on site. They suffered a storm of abuse, airborne spit-balls, and heavy objects whilst waiting for back up. The whole rumble ended swiftly when riot vans swept through the cat litter of family protestors using their kids as a frontline defence. At the back, a two-man team with a pickup truck winched up the vehicles, dragged them out, and impounded them. By the time the gypsies figured out what was going on, a half dozen 4x4s and their caravans had been removed. Even the guard dogs had been tranquillised and caged off to the animal shelter. Rumours spread and people fled to the back to save their homes only for the same tactic to begin at the front. The entire camp realised their safe-haven was over, jumped in their vehicles, and wheel-spun off the site in the direction of the by-pass. It all took less than an hour from the moment the court order was delivered. By daybreak, the place was as silent as it had been for twenty-years previous.

After Amit's update, coffee quench, and fist-bump goodbye, a whole hour needed to be killed before it was acceptable to ring Dixel's doorbell and collect his stuff. Until then greyscale commuters of all shapes and sizes dropped like Latte-holding Tetris pieces into queues for the train station.

A few homeless people stumbled against the flow towards their daytime sleeping spots. Living on the street level was a whole different ball game. They had their living room in public, their bedroom, their toilet, their dining room, all of it. A shouting match from one end of their house to the other was nothing, and if your ears got in the way, too bad. Good luck to anyone who used the *I pay my taxes* argument. The group of stragglers, passed by a man sleeping under two layers of cardboard and a Salvation Army blanket, in a shop entrance. They didn't even stop. Maybe this one was new and hadn't earned their place? Maybe this one was knocked out on meth or slaughtered on cider. The guy stirred a little when a dog approached and sniffed his face. A filthy hand flicked out from under his head and waved the mutt away. The hood of his jacket shifted, and Ethan noticed something familiar. It was Reed. Joel—with a flat—Reed. Ethan kept his distance and tried to figure out why he'd crashed in shop entrance instead of staying in the warm, dry four walls he'd been blessed with.

Kirsty should have taken him to the flat. Maybe it didn't happen? Plans can change, but she was certain it was all signed and sealed. Ethan still had the leaflet in his pocket from when Reed discarded it at the caravan. The property was about ten minutes' walk, and a visit would kill some time. He had no idea what a visit would tell him, but there was a chance that the previous tenant hadn't vacated. By the time he reached the Osbourne Way flats, the door to the block was open, and the landlord was letting a plumber inside.

'He told me he'd changed his mind. The paperwork was all in his name and I had the keys for him. But he wouldn't take them.'

'Why?'

'You'll have to ask him that.' The landlord went inside. 'It's still available if you can talk him into it.'

It took all of zero seconds to get on the phone to Heston. 'Sorry to wake you, but I need a favour.'

• • •

That afternoon the leisure centre had its gates back in place, and a new padlock. The gap in the hedge was still there and a brand-new caravan sat in the same spot where Reed's van had burnt down.

El Gato had won the contract after all. Bryon excelled at business development more than he realised. The council awarded Infinite Security the contract overnight as no other company saw it coming to bid. El Gato took the fastest handshake route possible to get a man on site. And that man was Bryon, of course, as not even he could turn down a double-time day-rate.

Bryon was sat outside, tired, bemused, and pissed with himself. 'I thought I resigned,' he said, 'but it wasn't even mentioned.'

'But that's good, right? You didn't have anything to go to yet, anyway.'

'Doesn't matter. I still wanted out.'

'Do you still want to quit?' Ethan said.

'Damn right, I do.' Bryon got up and paced around the dirt scuffing his feet like a grumpy child. 'What are the chances of finding a reliable replacement?' then, 'Your friend, by the way, I found out who he is. Bryon handed over a few printouts of some results. Ethan quickly read through the headlines.

'He's not well,' Bryon said.

'Oh, I know that, but the rest...' Ethan read some more. 'I kind of guessed, but this confirms it.

Thanks.' Ethan took off his backpack and pulled out a box—the BT Wi-Fi Shoebox. 'I got this. Can you set it up for me?'

'Sure.' Ethan had already started to walk back across the field. 'You're not staying to skate?'

'I want to, but I can't. I've got a lot to do.'

22

FISHING FOR A QUICK CHOP

Office C26 at N27 had a reputation for performing lobotomies. Whilst the rest of the building crackled with activity, more than usual, the corridor to Ethan's compulsory HR meeting stank of dead air. The synthetic carpet stored enough static to electrocute any survivors. Inside the room, two suited women sat at the opposite end of the table, he recognised neither of them. They smiled as he sat.

He brushed the top his head with his hand and leant on the desk.

'Mr Wares.' A fifties woman with tired skin and the makeup of a twenty-year-old pulled an A4 white envelope from a stack beside her. It had his name on it. 'No doubt you're aware of the changes in the company by this stage, however, we want to assure you that this is just an options package. Your performance over the last year has been exceptional and there's no reason to be concerned about your future in the company.' She handed him the envelope and ticked his name off a long list.

He couldn't see Heston's name on it. 'That's it?'

She left her hand covering the list. 'Unless you have any questions for us?'

'No.' Ethan stood. There was another list to her right, but he couldn't read any of the upside-down names.

'You don't want to open the envelope?' The woman looked surprised. 'We might be able to help you consider your options?'

'Am I fired?'

'No. Not at all.'

'Is that the list of people you're firing?'

The second woman stopped writing in her notepad. 'We've got lots of people to speak to today. It's not something you should worry about. Your contract and benefits will continue for another year.'

'Maybe I care about some of the others?'

'That's great to hear, Mr Wares. Caring is why Human Resources exists.'

Never in a million years.

On the second floor, Ethan found Dixel sat on the edge of a desk hugging a coffee. Across the room tearful ex-employees packed away their things into boxes. Normally, redundant staff were given notice, but those at mid-level with access to sensitive material, competitors, and client contact details had to leave immediately. All the clauses were tucked away in the Terms & Conditions of their contract no-one read called, *Privacy & Security*.

'Fired?' he asked

'They're not fired.' She blew on her coffee and watched a tearful couple pack up their things. 'They're still valued, but just not required. It's different.'

'Like a flesh-eating disease with a cute name or Rabies with a smile.'

She picked some dried chewing gum off her shoe with his opinion. 'Redundancy is different. I would call it an opportunity to find something better. They'll have a nice cheque.'

'They haven't been here long enough. They'll be lucky to get two months of wages, and even that will be taxed.'

Dixel noticed Ethan's envelope. 'You haven't opened yours yet?'

He shrugged.

She pulled up the latest report on her iPad. 'Have you seen these?' The figures compared to last week are down fifty-per cent.

'I'm not surprised. No-one wants to watch pool skating. I told them that.'

'The edit was good, though.'

'How did Ricard's edit do?'

'You don't want to know.'

That crackle of activity stirred again as fresh legs entered the room and made their way into the conference room.

'Are you staying around for Blacker's speech?' she asked. 'It's on now and I've heard he's a big fan of your work.' A wry smile lifted the crease of her mouth as she took another sip of coffee.

He felt the USB stick from Dennis' CCTV footage of the true Blacker in his pocket. 'Our company saviour? I might see how long I can bear it.'

'That's the spirit. Team player!'

Moments later, more beard oil aficionados and latte drinkers giggled into the hall. Dixel filtered in too, though Ethan chose to hold back, opting for a *last-in, first-out* approach. In minutes the hall was jammed, and he couldn't see a damn thing, so he took the ugly climb one floor up to the office above the conference hall.

This soulless room had no other purpose than to oversee the minions. The floor to ceiling window, as wide as a goalmouth, showed a rainbow of happiness below clapping with every pause as Blacker welcomed them. His speech about the future of the company rolled out like a twenty-year-old cognac, practised and perfect, premium quality bile. He praised the wonderful format, spoke of nurturing talent, emphasised their competitive edge, and gave his vision of the next twelve months.

It all sounded legit.

The office had a speaker system for company announcements, but everyone knew it was the annoying equivalent of a lifeguard with a whistle. The system was also idiot-proof. If someone inserted a USB stick with a video on it, they wouldn't have to scroll through menus and load up an app, it would appear on the screen immediately with a play button. N27s developers knew how to cater to the technologically illiterate who measured their success with the number of meetings per day and smiles per hour.

Ethan took out the USB stick from his pocket, pushed it into the tannoy system, and a frozen image of Blacker on his call appeared.

There was always a chance the clip wouldn't play: the format could have been wrong, the speakers off, the volume down, or the video link might not be enabled for some reason. A million things could prevent showing everyone that Blacker was bullshitting. The only way to find out was to tap the screen. It was just a piece of glass after all. It wouldn't be his fault that there just happened to be a play button underneath his finger. The office door wasn't locked so anyone could storm in and shut off the machine. HR wouldn't even need to shoulder barge the door or dive across the room to save their beloved leader. Another round of applause came from downstairs.

He pressed the play button.

The screen flicked into life. Initially, Blacker didn't notice until the audio began. Everyone turned to the huge image of the grainy office on the wall. It took a few seconds until he recognised himself, a flush of fear kicked through his veins, a knot of questions and answers jostled for order as he tried to plan an escape from the stage. The chaotic cycle of professional death manifested. The truth shifted beneath him as he realised what he was seeing, and a flicker of contained rage made him shift his weight to another foot.

The room silently listened to the black and white figure pace around the office, calling out incompetent people, threatening to slash entire departments, contradicting himself, shortening time frames, laughing. The laughing was the worst. The chaos Ethan imagined didn't arrive. No-one shouted *liar* or booed him off the stage, no-one threatened him or chucked their drinks at his head. Blacker looked to his left for someone to cut the feed. Ethan checked the door; no-one ran through it to wrestle him away from the machine.

The next stage of professional death kicked in: bargaining.

Blacker smiled, laughed, frowned, and calmly

dismissed everything people had just seen and heard come out of his mouth. That takes some balls. You don't get to be MD of a company without being able to talk your way out of trouble. He laughed again and focussed on specific people in the audience to crack a joke, and eventually, they laughed too. The nervous kind which didn't pinch the eyes.

Ethan pulled the USB stick out of the machine, flipped it over in his fingers a few times, then dropped it in the bin on his way out of the office.

By the time he got back into the lobby outside the conference room, people had already begun filing out. Dixel stopped Ethan just as he was leaving the floor. She was a little out of breath or excited, but happy too.

'You've got to hear this,' she said. 'A video of Blacker bad-mouthing the whole company just played on the projector. You should have seen it.'

Ethan nodded and started walking on.

'Wait.' She grabbed his sleeve and pushed him out into the stairwell. 'You did that, didn't you? Why?'

'Because he stank like out-of-date fish. I did him a favour. He can start with a clean sheet now, but judging what I've seen so far, he'll probably wriggle out of it.'

'Oh, he did that already. He said it was a clip

from another company recorded months ago. I think most people bought it.'

'I wouldn't be too sure of that.' Ethan pointed at a group gathered in the shape of hushed gossip, cupping their mouths to stop all the OMG's from falling out. 'I think people figured it out.'

23

FLAT SCREAM TV

Six months of dust on the top edge of Ethan's 72-inch TV caught his eye during a breather carrying it up to his new home. He swept it clean with a dry index finger. Heston's insurance money had paid out. £234,000 in total; a life-changing sum of money, however, he wasn't quite ready to celebrate with a Ferrari. It was hard to not jibe him with spending ideas, but Heston, level-headed as always, knew he had a long road of rehabilitation ahead.

'Thanks for holding this for me.' Ethan rolled the ball of dust between the tips of his fingers and flicked it over the railing to fall three flights of stairs to the floor. 'I'm surprised it lasted so long. I thought it might have got "damaged" by now.'

'No chance.' Heston stood at the top of the stairwell. 'I've had enough of dealing with Insurance companies. Besides, SmartHome still own this, right? I don't think you'll be free of your contract if a board accidentally went through the screen.'

'I still can't thank you enough.' Ethan took one uneasy step after another up the final flight, as Heston watched the corners.

'For what?'

'The flat.'

'The best gift I could give myself is getting you off my sofa and out of my house. All you've got to do is pay the rest of the bills. I'm only covering the first year's rent.'

'I know you like your privacy and all, but when are you going to tell me about this new girlfriend?' Ethan set the monitor down on the top step to pause for breath.

'It's just new. I don't want to,' Heston searched for the word, 'jeopardise my chances.'

'But she's moving in. That's a big deal.'

The noise of a drill bit crunched into the living room wall. 'Let's just get this thing inside, can we?' Heston stood back and gave Ethan more room. Dixel had just finished screwing the TV bracket to the wall. She raised her safety glasses and wiped her hand on the front of her dungarees. 'We're ready to go,' she said.

'Can I check it?' Ethan asked.

'Nope.' She placed the drill into its case and threw a plastic bracket to him. 'You can fit that to the back of the TV.'

Ethan lined up the holes and started spinning the small bolts into the fitting. 'Can you believe he still won't tell me anything about who he's dating?'

'Yes,' Dixel said. 'And I don't blame him. Have you changed the locks yet?'

'I'm doing that tomorrow.' Heston went to the window and put his hand on the glass. 'This is a single pane; it might get cold during the winter.'

'Don't worry,' Ethan said. 'The bills are fixed so I'll be burning through the Ozone layer to keep it warm.'

A familiar face came through the gate below. 'Your old mate Ren is coming.'

Ethan looked out of the window and saw Ren in a courier shirt carrying a parcel up the main path to the block. 'Ah, shit.'

Heston's phone beeped with an incoming message. 'I'll go shut the front door so your mate, sorry, ex-mate, doesn't realise you live here yet.'

Ethan returned to his TV fixing, 'Yeah you do that then tell your girlfriend I'll look forward to meeting her, one day.'

'Why don't you leave him alone?' Dixel picked up some junk mail and binned it.

'He's fine.'

'He's obviously not ready to share his relationship details yet.' She washed her hands and dried them with a towel. 'When exactly are you going to patch up your beef with your friends then?'

'I don't know if that's possible.'

'You should just apologise anyway; it doesn't even matter whether you're at fault or not. You need to show regret and the value of restoring the friendship. It's not about who's to blame and who said or did whatever, besides, apologies get harder the longer you leave it."

'I know,' Ethan said, 'but not right now.'

Heston returned with a free newspaper. 'Well, guess who made the front cover of the local?' He put the Journal on the table.

Ethan picked it up and saw a photo of Reed, iPad in one hand, a puppy in the other, with El Gato and Kirsty Sapsford beside him. The headline said *Homeless Soldier Reunited with Troop After 10 years.* The article went on to say, *The soldier with PTSD lived at the leisure centre with the belief that his troop would return. He was reunited with them over video chat. His life had taken a turn for the worst when his caravan was burnt down, but reversed his misfortune after local entrepreneur, Edwardo Hermanez, employed him as a security guard for the site. Mr Hermanez told the Journal that he couldn't be happier to have Mr Reed on the team and was looking forward to utilising his skills for Infinite Security.*

'You did that?' Heston asked.

'I guess, I helped,' Ethan said. 'Bryon did the rest.'

Heston offered to give Dixel a lift back to her place. They packed up their things and left Ethan to it. For the first time in months, he finally had a place to himself and as soon as the lock clicked behind them, he sat on the sofa and tried to let himself accept that it was his.

The clock on the wall ticked away louder than he could bare after thirty seconds. He put his hands in his hoodie pocket and felt a business card. It was the therapist's details Reed had given him on the first day they met. That clock kept ticking and he felt it was getting louder. It certainly wasn't going to shut up. After another fifteen seconds, he got up, pulled the battery out, and threw it in the bin.

It didn't seem like five minutes of peace and tranquillity when the business card in his pocket niggled him again. He'd had enough of this anxiety. If it wasn't the clock, or the stairs at work, or confined spaces, it was something else. The doctor sent him away with useless advice, claiming it was stress-related and how he should have a holiday, and Google only came up with one answer: speaking to a professional. Ethan always thought they were for desperate people; besides, he spoke to people all the time, and nothing had helped him so far. Paying someone to listen just added to the worry instead of helping it. What does a therapist cost? Twenty, Fifty, A hundred pounds an hour? He didn't have that sort of money to blast. He threw the business card towards the dining room table where it banked around and landed by the window.

That TV still needed hanging.

With a little bit of fiddling, he managed to line up the bracket on the back and slot it into the catch on the wall. It looked pretty good up there, big and black, and reflective in the light. It took a few moments to scan all the stations until the audio popped, nice and clear, out of the speakers. He sat back and flicked through the schedule.

The buzzer went on his intercom.

'It's SmartHome repossessions,' the voice crackled through the system speaker. 'We're here to collect the TV for non-payment.'

It had taken approximately 24 hours after cancelling his direct debit for the company to mark him as a wanted man on their system.

'It's paid for.' Ethan released the button and returned to the sofa. The intercom cut in again.

'The payments have stopped so I'm afraid we need to take the TV back.'

A wildlife programme followed a Cheetah in South Africa stalking an Antelope across the Kenyan plains. The Repossessions team followed their recovery steps. In the section marked, *Collection*: a tick was added to the *No response* box.

The Cheetah froze, as the Antelope drank from a watering hole, before lifting its head momentarily. It returned to drink.

Attempted collection: another tick in the *No response* box.

The Cheetah pushed slowly through the bracken, crawling inches from the floor, eyes locked on its prey.

Explanation of Circumstances; *Claims the TV is paid for,* was scribbled in the Comments section.

Cut to a wide view of the watering hole: the Antelope stood at the water's edge, the Cheetah eased out from the bushes from behind, there was no-where for the prey to escape unless it cut across the water. The Antelope looked up again, sensing danger nearby.

Attempts to enter the building: *Met with swearing through the intercom.*

The two animals waited for each other to react. The Cheetah could have attacked but didn't. It toyed with the animal. The Antelope sniffed the breeze, then suddenly bolted.

Explanation of terms and conditions: *missed payments whilst in the Final Warning stages of communications would result in immediate action. Customer told the representative to sod off.*

Description of additional attempts to secure the items: *Told the customer that we'd notify the landlord of the premises and take proceedings to recover the monies owed through Rent Recovery or risk eviction.*

Ethan got up and unclipped the TV from the wall bracket. The power cable disconnected; the aerial lead dropped on the floor. He stood in the middle of the room with the front corner pointing towards the window and ran at it. The TV cut through the glass with a sparkling explosion, the bottom corner caught on the windowsill and sent the screen into a spin to the floor. The impact was less impressive. A heavy muffled tambourine of electronics and glass distorted under its weight. It landed on its side and fell onto its back. The second man from the recovery team walked out of the block entrance and looked up at the window to see Ethan looking down.

The men took photos of the damage and left the TV on the lawn. Within a couple of minutes, they shoved a copy of their paperwork through his letterbox and returned to their van.

Ethan calmed down whilst watching the men leave, then immediately regretted his actions. The smashed window, the gate, the road, the terrace houses across the road, a scaffolder on the roof took a break to fiddle with his radio, a seagull flew over and rested on the chimney. The view flattened for a moment, all depth was lost, the gull almost touched the clouds above its head. Those clouds brushed the desaturated ferns of the woods in the distance. A length of glass in the window stuck out like a knife. He wriggled it free from the cracked putty and examined the fragmented light against the sky. Its blade, clinical and clean, its weight, hardly noticeable. He tapped the piece on the edge of the windowsill and expected it to break. He tapped it again, much harder, then again, and again, until it broke into two long thin knives. The split ran directly under his thumb and sliced the skin which balled with blood. He stuck it in his mouth, sat on the chair by the table, and noticed the Therapists' business card on the floor.

'Hello,' he said when Loretta Deane's answerphone message ended. 'I think I need some help.'

BOOK 4: PUNCH DRUNK
SAMPLE

UP IN SMOKE

It was a cold and cloudy afternoon when Ethan slotted a spanner over his kingpin and spun it into a frictionless vortex. 'It doesn't fit.' He handed it back to Mike. 'You got any others?' He couldn't bash the kid, but what skater carries a 15mm? A wobble he could handle, but when things reach a Daewon level it's time to tighten up the slack.

Today's meet up was at the newly built plaza, that consisted of a foot high square block around a tree and nearly two on the far side. Brand new smooth concrete slabs covered the floor, and as soon as the fences came down, the skaters were all over it. The renovation of the old cobble-stone square of infinite insurance claims had been funded by a wealthy entrepreneur who recently moved into the area. The newspaper ink was still gossipy with the pledge to employ, invest, and expand operations of their honey production business. As far as the skaters were concerned, the real ball-ache came from the purchase of the Ubley Estate, as they had earmarked one of the barns for a winter indoor mini-ramp. That idea had now gone the way of the demolition in progress across the road.

A huge JCB bucket pulled a wall over from twenty feet up, which sent bricks and mortar crashing down into a pile of dust.

Mike's friend Kyle arrived and was immediately ribbed for wearing a pair of trousers several sizes too big everywhere except the legs. The kid kicked away their comments like a boss. Still, this was a fashion faux pas Ethan couldn't comprehend.

The bottoms were wide like the kids' influences and the turn-ups deep to match his bank balance.

Another sucker.

More rubble crashed from the building works.

'What do you think Ethe?' Mike pointed out Kyle's trousers. '£120.'

'They'd need to pay me that to wear them.'

'Are you going to that Nike event?' Mike asked. A premiere was happening in Bristol and everyone who was anyone was invited, which meant, as Ethan was the only anyone they knew, he must have had an offer.

'No chance,' he said. 'Screw Nike.'

'Can I have your invite?' Mike was ready for the rebuttal. His friends quickly followed and began bickering amongst themselves for the ticket as if it would manifest out of Ethan's pocket into their hands.

'It doesn't work like that. The ticket has my name on it. Besides, I didn't accept it.'

'Why not?' Fancy Trousers asked. 'I heard Nyjah was going to be there.' His friends scoffed at the unlikely appearance, but still, the kid hugged that rumour like a true fan. 'I'm going anyway,' he said. 'I just want to see who turns up and maybe get something autographed.'

'Imagine being on Nike,' another kid said. They all replied in unison at how dope it would be.

The digger bucket jammed itself into a wall and clanked backwards and forwards trying to dislodge something steel reinforced.

'How about I get my ticket changed to the name of the first person who lands a hardflip?'

'None of us can hardflip,' Mike said. But that didn't stop Fancy Trousers getting on his board to try it. Everyone else joined him, and eventually, Mike gave in and tried as well. Ethan left the grommets to it and took a roll around the ledges.

Too many people at the plaza in Fluro jackets was never a good sign. The workers who carried concrete dust in their boot grooves and under their fingernails were welcome; they had a job to do and could easily be ignored, but everyone carrying a clipboard was a problem. One such council officer took photos, measured areas, and noted issues. Ethan kept his distance, but not the younger skaters. A loose board from a hard-flip session rolled out and the officer politely stepped aside to let the kid retrieve it. Fancy Trousers gave up his hard-flip attempts first and started a manual roll train across the ledge towards the officer. Not a good move. Soon a board headed straight for the man's Achilles tendons again.

'Here's a bad slab.' Ethan guided the man away from the kids. The officer stood on the slab and tried to rock it with his weight. 'It's within our tolerances.'

'The edge is higher than the others.' Ethan pointed at the lip. 'These wheels find all imperfections.' But the officer stressed it wasn't an issue.

A van towing a mini digger pulled up onto the curb near the end of the high ledge. Three workmen got out.

'Have you got more work planned?' Ethan nodded in the workmen's direction.

'Not by us. They must be contractors working on the pelican crossing.'

The team lifted out blocks from the back of the trailer. The type designed to allow the blind to feel their way to the curb. The worst kind.

James from N27 research pulled up in a branded car.

Mike saw him first. 'Is that the location? Where are you going?' Mike asked.

'No idea,' Ethan replied. 'You asked me that last time and the answer is still the same.'

'I still don't get why they won't tell you.'

'I don't see the point in keeping it quiet either, but the marketing team want it all hush-hush.'

'Why? We'd still watch it,' Mike said, 'It'll probably make it better because we'd tell everyone.'

James didn't have a folder in his hands. 'I don't think you'll need a full briefing this time. You're skating that.' He pointed across the street to a six-stair handrail outside the Hives Honey shop.

'You're kidding?' People skated that rail all the time, but it was a one-hit-wonder cut off by the road and very little other options for lines. 'We've got a whole plaza here and they pick the Hives retail rail? How are people supposed to get excited?'

James shrugged. 'You'll have to get creative. And make it good because your stats have been slipping. Between you and me, Marketing is already dreaming up new ideas.'

'As long as they stick to adverts and whatever else they do. I don't want them anywhere near me.'

During Ethan's first week at N27, he was asked to come up with a hundred riding locations to pitch to management for the series. A hundred? In a small town like Ubley. That was asking a lot. The first ten were a breeze, and it took him another twenty-four hours to come up with another ten. Days passed getting creative to push the list to forty. The final squeeze involved searching maps to bring the list to fifty. This included the slightest bump-gap, buckled tarmac, couple of steps, and any random concrete slope which included the dull Hives rail. The results all ended up in a presentation which looked good on a big screen but was eighty per cent bullshit. He was promised most wouldn't make the final list. That was the first lie of many.

Ethan skated off, annoyed. James hung about for a bit wondering if he was returning for a conversation or questions until he figured he wasn't and left.

The workmen were the more immediate problem as they set down their tools right in front of the pelican crossing, blocking the landing of the big ledge. A few of the kids had already complained, but the workers didn't care. The session would be ruined once those slabs were set. Luckily, their arrival meant his spanner options increased. They were happy to open the lid of the toolbox and let him find the right size for his trucks. Whilst the workers were occupied, Ethan took the fattest spanner he could find and flipped the lid of the mini digger's battery compartment. A large spark jumped from the unit as he dropped it on top of the terminals. He shut the lid and finished tightening his trucks, then skated off to the other side of the plaza.

He ollied into a backside 50-50 and hopped out, then carved around to the next ledge and bonked a quick little crook off the corner. He no-complied around to fakie and half-cab flipped himself straight again and tre-flipped a traffic cone on its side. The workers shooed the kids away and a brief mouthy exchange followed. It was a bad move, but understandable. They could see what Ethan could: the men were wrecking the day, the roll, and the ledge.

One of the workers unhooked the back of the trailer and pulled out the ramps for the mini digger. It was going to be an interesting few minutes. As soon as they turned the ignition, a crack of electricity popped and a plume of burnt plastic smoke wafted out of the cab. The electrics had completely blown. Two other workmen walked around to the cab and waved the smoke from their face. They tried the ignition again, but it was dead. Within minutes of arriving, they started lifting the blocks back into the trailer.

'They're leaving?' Mike said.

'It looks like you'll be having a good session, after all.'

OTHER TITLES

Read the rest of the Ethan Wares Skateboard
series now:

Book 1: The Blocks
Book 2: Abandoned
Book 4: Punch Drunk
Book 5: Nutbar DIY

AUTHOR'S NOTE

If you liked this story and would be interested in reading more, you can join my mailing list at https://skatefiction.co.uk and become one of my beta readers who get early access to new stories, give feedback, and receive reader copies in advance.

If you loved the book, please leave a positive review wherever you purchased it as this is the main way good books spread and help people discover me.

Thanks - Mark

ABOUT THE AUTHOR

Mark Mapstone is a UK skateboarder, writer, and author of the Ethan Wares Skateboard Series books.

After discovering there were no fiction books written for skateboarders with realistic skateboarding in them, and being qualified with a degree in creative writing from the prestigious Bath Spa University, Mark decided he was perfectly positioned to cater this audience.

In-between road-trips, an infinite Instagram feed of videos to watch, and discovering bruises on himself which he has no-idea how they got there, Mark uses his knowledge of the current skateboarding world to create exciting and authentic stories which every skateboarder goes through daily.

Follow Mark on Instagram: @7plywood.